**2ND** EDITION

Starter
Students' Book

with DVD-ROM

Frances Eales • Steve Oakes

CONTENTS

DVD-ROM: **BBC** DVD CLIPS AND SCRIPTS   ◉) BBC INTERVIEWS AND SCRIPTS   ▶ CLASS AUDIO AND SCRIPTS

CONTENTS

LISTENING/DVD	SPEAKING	WRITING
listen to people say *hello*	introduce yourself	learn to use capital letters
	ask questions about people	
listen to people give personal information	give personal information	
BBC **Around the World**: watch a BBC programme about people around the world	speak about yourself and your country	write a personal introduction
listen to someone talk about photos	talk about photos of family and friends	learn to use contractions
listen to people talk about their daily routines	check information about people	
listen to people making suggestions	suggest things to do	
BBC **The Royal Wedding: Willliam and Catherine**: watch a BBC programme about a royal wedding	talk about five people in your life	write a description of five people in your life
listen to conversations between students	ask about objects	
	talk about possessions	use linkers *and, but*
listen to people in a café	order food and drink	
BBC **Francesco's Mediterranean Voyage**: watch a BBC programme about a famous market	buy things in a market	write about a market
listen to people talk about life in the USA	find things in common	use linkers
	find differences in pictures	
listen to people tell the time	tell the time	
BBC **Amish: a secret life**: watch a BBC programme about an unusual family	do a class survey	write a short report about lifestyles
listen to people talk about what drives them crazy	discuss bad habits	
	talk about what you eat	use to linkers to sequence
listen to a tourist asking questions	ask for tourist information	
BBC **How to feed your kids**: watch a BBC programme about children and food	discuss what food and drink to take to a desert island	write a forum entry

CONTENTS

CONTENTS

NUMBERS 1–10

1 A Match the words in the box with the numbers.

> ~~zero~~ nine three one seven ten four two
> eight five six

0 _zero_	**4** _____	**8** _____
1 _____	**5** _____	**9** _____
2 _____	**6** _____	**10** _____
3 _____	**7** _____	

B ▶ L1 Listen and check. Then listen and repeat.

C ▶ L2 Listen and write the numbers.

D Work in pairs and take turns. Student A: say a number. Student B: say the next number.

A: five *B:* six
B: zero *A:* one

INTERNATIONAL ENGLISH

2 A Match the words in the box with photos 1–6.

> DVD *1* phone hotel football bus chocolate

B ▶ L3 Listen and check. Then listen and repeat.

C Work in pairs. Write five more international words.

▷ page 138 **PHOTOBANK**

CLASSROOM LANGUAGE

3 A ▶ L4 Listen and underline the correct word.

Conversation 1
A: OK, Antonio. ¹*What's* /*Is* 'libro' in English?
B: Sorry, I ²*not/don't* know.
A: It's 'book'.
B: Can you ³*write/say* it, please?
A: Yes …

Conversation 2
A: OK. Open your books, please.
B: Sorry, I ⁴*no/don't* understand.
A: Open, like this.
B: Which ⁵*page/number*?
A: Page eight.
B: Can you ⁶*repeat/write* that, please?
A: Yes, page eight.
B: Thank you.

B Work in pairs and take turns. Practise the conversations.

▷ page 138 **PHOTOBANK**

speakout TIP

Start a phrasebook. Write useful phrases, e.g. *Hello, Hi, Good morning, Good afternoon, Good evening, Good night.*

1

hello

RE ARE YOU FROM? p8   ARRIVALS p11   HOW DO YOU SPELL...? p14   AROUND THE WORLD p16

SPEAKING 1.1 Introduce yourself 1.2 Ask questions about people 1.3 Give personal information 1.4 Speak about yourself and your country

LISTENING 1.1 Listen to people say *hello* 1.3 Listen to people give personal information 1.4 Watch a BBC programme about people around the world

READING 1.2 Read descriptions of people arriving at an airport

WRITING 1.1 Learn to use capital letters 1.4 Write a personal introduction

BBC INTERVIEWS

◁)) Where are you from?

7

G *be: I/you*
P sentence stress; word stress
V countries

LISTENING

1 A ▶ 1.1 Listen and match conversations 1–3 with photos A–C.

1 _____   2 _____   3 _____

B Listen again and match the person with the country and city.

1	Carmen		Dublin
		Australia	Cork
2	Katie	Ireland	Madrid
		Spain	Barcelona
3	Steve		Sydney
			Melbourne

GRAMMAR

BE: I/YOU

2 A Complete the tables with *'m* and *are*. Use the audio script on page 154 to help you.

| I | *'m* | Carmen. |
| | | from Spain. |

| Where | _____ | you | from? |
| | _____ | you | from Sydney? |

| Yes, | I | am. |
| No, | | _____ not. |

B ▶ 1.2 **SENTENCE STRESS** Listen and underline the stressed words.

I'm <u>Carmen</u>.

C Listen again and repeat the sentences.

▷ page 118 **LANGUAGEBANK**

3 A Complete the conversations with *'m* or *are*.

Conversation 1
A: Hello, I ¹ _'m_ Janet.
B: Hi, I ² _____ Oscar. Nice to meet you.
A: You too. Where ³ _____ you from?
B: I ⁴ _____ from Colombia.
A: Oh, where in Colombia?
B: From Bogotá.

Conversation 2
A: Hello, I ⁵ _____ Kasia.
B: Hi, I ⁶ _____ Peter.
A: Nice to meet you.
B: You too. Where ⁷ _____ you from?
A: I ⁸ _____ from Poland.
B: ⁹ _____ you from Warsaw?
A: No, I'm not. I'm from Gdańsk.

B ▶ 1.3 Listen and check.

C Work in pairs and practise the conversations.

D Work in pairs and talk about your name, country and town/city.

A: Hello, I'm …
B: Hi, I'm …

1 Moscow

2 Beijing

3 London

4 Brasília

5 Washington D.C.

6 Berlin

7 Ankara

8 Rome

VOCABULARY

COUNTRIES

4 A Match the countries in the box with pictures 1–8 above.

| Brazil 4 Italy the USA China Russia Turkey the UK Germany |

B ▶ 1.4 Listen and check.

C WORD STRESS Listen again and underline the stress in the countries. Then listen and repeat.

Russia

D Work in pairs. Student A: ask *Where's … ?* Student B: say the country.

A: *Where's Berlin?*
B: *It's in Germany.*

speakout TIP

Write new words in your phrasebook and underline the stress, e.g. *China*, *the USA*.

▷ page 139 **PHOTOBANK**

WRITING

CAPITAL LETTERS

5 A Underline the capital letters in sentences a)–f) in the conversation.

a) I'm Karin.

b) Hi, I'm Tony Ferrari.

c) Are you from Italy?

d) No, I'm American. I'm from Washington D.C.

e) Are you a student?

f) Yes, I am.

B Match rules 1–6 with sentences a)–f) above.

| RULES | Use capital letters for:
1 the name of a person *a, b*
2 a country
3 a city
4 *I*
5 the first word in a sentence
6 nationalities |

C Find and correct the mistakes with capitals in messages below.

1 hi, i'm bao, and i'm a teacher in china.

2 hi, i'm sylvia. i'm russian. are You from beijing?

3 no, i'm from shanghai. are you from moscow ?

4 yes, i am. i'm a student.

6 A Work in pairs. Write a chat message to your partner.

Hi, I'm …

B Swap messages. Answer the message.

A: *Hi, I'm …*
B: *Hi, I'm …*

SPEAKING

7 A Write a country and a city from the country.

Italy – Venice

B Work in groups and take turns. Guess the cities.

A: *Where are you from?*
B: *I'm from Italy.*
C: *Oh, you're Italian. Are you from Rome?*
B: *No, I'm not.*
A: *Are you from … ?*

F be: he/she/it
P word stress
V jobs

VOCABULARY

JOBS

1 A Write the jobs in the box under pictures 1–8.

> a teacher   a doctor   a taxi driver   a waiter
> an actor   a businessman/businesswoman
> a singer   an engineer

1
_____

2
_____

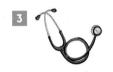
3
_____

4
_____

5
_____

6
_____

7
_____

8
_____

B ▶ 1.5   Listen and check.

C WORD STRESS Listen again and underline the stressed syllable. Then listen and repeat.

2 A Look at the conversation. Underline the correct alternative in the rules.

A: Are you a teacher?

B: No, I'm a student, an English student. Are you an actor?

A: No, I'm a singer, an Italian singer.

> **RULES**
> **1** Use *a/an* with words starting with vowels (*a, e, i, o, u*).
> **2** Use *a/an* with words starting with consonants (*b, c, d* …).

B Work in pairs and take turns. Student A: say a job and a nationality. Student B: say *a* or *an*.

A: doctor, Spanish
B: a Spanish doctor

C Work with other students. Student A: mime a job. Other students: guess the job.

B: Are you an engineer?
A: No, I'm not.
C: Are you a doctor?
A: Yes, I am.

▷ **page 139 PHOTOBANK**

welcome to
JFK
AIRPORT

Sonia Conti is a student from Italy. 'I'm a business student at Columbia University'

'Is it a good university?'

'Yes, it is. It's very good for my English too. I love it.'

READING

3 A Work in pairs. Look at the photos of people at JFK airport, New York. Who is a tourist?

B Read the texts and check your answer.

C Complete the table with the correct information.

Name	Job	Country	First time in New York
Wei Zhang			
	actor/waiter		
		Brazil	
			no

Wei Zhang is a Chinese computer engineer.

'I'm from Beijing but I'm not here on business. I'm here on holiday. It's my first time in New York.'

Maria Silva is from Brazil. She's an English teacher. She's in New York for an International Teachers' Conference. 'It isn't my first time in the US but it's my first time in New York. I'm very happy to be here.'

Jack Brown is an actor from Sydney, Australia.

'I'm a TV actor in Australia, but here in New York I'm a waiter in a restaurant. The people are nice. New York's a good city for actors.'

GRAMMAR

BE: HE/SHE/IT

4 A Underline the verb *be* in the sentences.

1 Wei Zhang <u>is</u> a computer engineer.
2 She<u>'s</u> an English teacher.
3 It <u>isn't</u> my first time in England.
4 <u>Is</u> it a good university? Yes, it <u>is</u>.

B Complete the tables.

He She It	<u>is</u> / 's / is not / <u>isn't</u>	from Italy.

_____	he/she/it	from China? / a teacher? / your first time here?
Yes,	he/she/it	is.
No,		_____.

Where	_____	he/she/it	from?

C ▶ 1.6 Listen and write sentences 1–6. Then listen and repeat.

▷ page 118 **LANGUAGEBANK**

5 A Add *'s* (*is*) in ten places.

1 Ellie Turner'ˢ from Liverpool in the UK. She a teacher at UCL. It a big university in London. She in New York for a conference.

2 Yong-Joon from Korea. He a taxi driver in Seoul, the capital. He in New York on holiday. He happy to be here.

3 Monika a businesswoman from Ottawa in Canada. She in New York on business.

B Add words to make questions.

1 Ellie / the UK?
Is Ellie from the UK?
2 she / doctor?
3 UCL / New York?
4 Yong-Joon / Japan?
5 he / New York / on holiday?
6 Ottawa / Canada?

C Match answers a)–f) with questions 1–6 above.

a) No, it isn't.
b) Yes, he is.
c) Yes, she is. *1*
d) No, he isn't.
e) Yes, it is.
f) No, she isn't.

D Cover the answers above. Work in pairs and ask and answer questions 1–6.

SPEAKING

6 Work in pairs and take turns. Student A: turn to page 148. Student B: turn to page 150.

1.3)) HOW DO YOU SPELL …?

F giving personal information
P the alphabet; sentence stress
V the alphabet

VOCABULARY

THE ALPHABET

Aa Bb Cc Dd
Ee Ff Gg Hh
Ii Jj Kk Ll
Mm Nn Oo Pp
Qq Rr Ss Tt
Uu Vv Ww Xx
Yy Zz

1 A ▶ 1.7 Listen and repeat the letters.

B SOUNDS: the alphabet Write the missing letters in the correct place in the table.

Sound	Letter
1 n<u>a</u>me /eɪ/	A H J __
2 m<u>ee</u>t /iː/	B C _ _ _ _ _ _
3 t<u>e</u>n /e/	F L _ _ _ _ _ _
4 n<u>i</u>ne /aɪ/	I __
5 n<u>o</u> /əʊ/	O
6 y<u>ou</u> /uː/	Q U __
7 c<u>ar</u> /aː/	R

C ▶ 1.8 Listen and check. Then listen and repeat.

2 A Work in pairs. Student A: turn to page 148. Student B: turn to page 150.

B Work in pairs and take turns. Student A: turn to page 139 and spell four countries, nationalities or jobs. Student B: write the words. Student A: check the spelling.

A

FUNCTION

GIVING PERSONAL INFORMATION

3 A ▶ 1.9 Listen and match conversations 1–3 with photos A–C.

1 _____
2 _____
3 _____

B Listen again and complete the information.

	First name	Surname	Room number
1		*Thompson*	
2			
3			

4 A Complete the form with the words in the box.

~~First name~~ Email address Nationality Surname Phone number

Riverside gym

Membership form

First name:	Michael
	Thompson
	American
	0532 419
	mike@bmail.com

B Underline the correct alternative.

1 **A:** What's /are your first name?
  B: Michael.

2 **A:** How do you spell/say that?
  B: M-i-c-h-a-e-l.

3 **A:** What's your phone number?
  B: It's ow/oh five three two, four one nine.

4 **A:** What's your email address?
  B: It's mike at/it bmail point/ dot com.

C Listen again to the first conversation and check your answers.

D ▶ 1.10 SENTENCE STRESS Listen and underline the stressed words. Then listen and repeat.

1 What's your phone number?

2 What's your email address?

▷ page 118 **LANGUAGEBANK**

5 A Write a phone number and an email address.

B Work in pairs and take turns. Ask your partner for their phone number and email address.

A: What's your phone number?
B: It's 382 7492.

LEARN TO

CHECK SPELLING

6 A ▶ 1.11 Listen to conversation and underline the stressed letters.

  A: And your first name?
  B: It's Allen.
  A: A-l-l … is it a-n?
  B: No, e. E as in England. A-l-l-e-n.

speakout **TIP**

Some names of letters are difficult, for example Y, J and G, I and E. Write words to help you remember, e.g. Y as in yes, J as in Japan. Do this for G, I and E below.

_____ _____ _____

B Work in pairs and take turns. Correct the spelling.

Not correct	Correct	Not correct	Correct
1 Obdul	Abdul	4 Geanette	Jeanette
2 Cinthia	Cynthia	5 Eves	Yves
3 Neal	Neil	6 Jeff	Geoff

A: Is it O-b-d-u-l?
B: No, A. A as in Australia. A-b-d-u-l. Is it C-i-n-t-h-i-a?

SPEAKING

7 Ask three students about their personal information and complete the tables below. Use Exercise 4B to help.

	Student 1	Student 2	Student 3
First name			
Surname			
Nationality			
Phone number			
Email address			

A Santiago, Chile

B Finland

C Oman

D Kuala Lumpur, Malaysia

E Malaysia

F Canada

DVD PREVIEW

1 A Work in pairs. Match the nouns in the box with the photos.

> a city *A, D*   a mountain   a river   a village
> a building   the countryside   a beach   the sea

B Work in pairs. Find three pairs of opposites in the box below.

> old   small   beautiful   new   cold   big   hot

C Work in pairs and take turns. Student A: choose one photo and say one adjective and one noun from the boxes above. Student B: say the place.

A: *beautiful countryside*   **B:** *Canada?*   **A:** *Yes!*
B: *an old building*   **A:** *Chile?*   **B:** *No …*

2 Read the programme information and underline the countries.

◑)) Around The World BBC

In this programme, people from around the world answer the questions: Who are you? Where are you from? What's your job? We speak to Kustaa in Finland, Mizna in Oman, Pablo in Chile, Aisha in Malaysia and Eric in Canada.

DVD VIEW

3 A Watch the DVD and number the places in the order you see them.

a) British Columbia, Canada
b) Santiago, Chile   *1*
c) Helsinki, Finland
d) Kuala Lumpur, Malaysia
e) Muscat, Oman

B Work in pairs. Which things from Exercise 1A are in the places?

Chile – a city, a building, a mountain

C Watch the DVD again to check your answers.

D Work in pairs and underline the correct alternative. Then watch the DVD again to check your answers.

1 Santiago, Chile is *old/old and new.*
2 The mountains in Chile are *hot/cold.*
3 Eric is a *waiter/driver* on a train.
4 Mizna is a *teacher/student* at university.
5 She is from a *city/village.*
6 In Finland, the countryside is good for *winter/summer* sport.
7 Kuala Lumpur is a(n) *old/new* city.
8 Aisha is a(n) *shop/office* assistant.

E Discuss with other students. Which country is your favourite? Why?

speakout you and your country

4 A ▶ 1.12 Listen and answer the questions for Catarina.

Name: Catarina

1 Where are you from? *Positano in Italy*
2 Is it big? _____
3 Is it old? _____
4 What's your job? _____
5 Where's your job? _____
6 Is English important for you? _____
7 What's good about (name of city or country)?
   _____

B Listen again and tick the key phrases you hear.

> **KEY PHRASES**
>
> It's a/an [Spanish/Irish/Italian/…] name.
> I'm a/an [teacher/hotel receptionist/engineer/…] at …
> [Dublin/Positano/It/…] is [a city/a town/a village] in …
> It's/It isn't very [small/big/beautiful/hot/…].
> The countryside [here/in Ireland/in …] is very beautiful.
> I really love it here.

5 A Prepare to talk about yourself. Write your answers to the questions in Exercise 4A. Use the key phrases to help.

B Work in pairs and take turns. Student A: ask student B questions. Student B: answer and give extra information.

writeback a personal introduction

6 A Read the personal introduction for a class blog. Tick the information you can find in the introduction.

1 name ✓
2 nationality
3 email address
4 job
5 city
6 country
7 *Hello* and *Goodbye*
8 languages

> **About me**
>
> **Rita Peterson's blogspot**
>
> Hi, or 'Hallo' in German. I'm Rita Petersen and I'm from Germany. I'm a businesswoman with Volkswagen. I speak German and English in my job.
>
> I'm from Berlin, the capital city of Germany. Berlin is a big city with a mix of old and new buildings. The countryside in Germany is beautiful, with mountains and rivers.
>
> 5 comments

B Write a personal introduction. Use the introduction above to help. Write 50–70 words.

G BE: I/YOU

1 A Complete the conversation with the words in the box.

> ~~Are~~   'm   I   am   in   you
> not   five

A: ¹ _Are_ you from Beijing?
B: No, I ² _____ not.
A: Are ³ _____ from Madrid?
B: Yes, I ⁴ _____.
A: Are you ⁵ _____ Mexico City now?
B: No, I'm ⁶ _____.
A: Are you number ⁷ _____?
B: Yes, ⁸ _____ am.

B Work in pairs and take turns. Student A: choose a sentence from 1–6 below. Student B: ask questions and guess the sentence.

1 I'm from Beijing. I'm in London now.
2 I'm from Madrid. I'm in Mexico City now.
3 I'm from New York. I'm in Tokyo now.
4 I'm from New York. I'm in London now.
5 I'm from Madrid. I'm in Tokyo now.
6 I'm from Beijing. I'm in Mexico City now.

B: Are you from New York?
A: Yes, I am.
B: Are you in Tokyo?
A: No, I'm not.
B: Number 4!

V COUNTRIES

2 A Work in pairs. Write the countries.

1 São Paulo B_razil_
2 Hamburg G _____
3 St. Petersburg R_____
4 Milan I _____
5 Shanghai C _____
6 Istanbul T _____

B Write five countries and a city in each country.

China – Beijing

C Work in pairs and take turns. Student A: ask about one of your cities. Student B: answer.

A: Where's Beijing?
B: It's in China.
A: That's right.

V JOBS

3 A Add the vowels (a, e, i, o ,u) to the jobs.

1 w__ __t__r
2 t_x__ dr__v__r
3 __ng__n__ __r
4 d__ct__r
5 __ct__r
6 t__ __ch__r
7 s__ng__r
8 b__s__n__ssw__m__n

B Work in groups. Student A: choose a job from 1–8 or from page 139. Other students: close your books and guess the job.

B: Are you a businesswoman?
A: No, I'm not.
C: Are you a doctor?
A: Yes, I am.

G BE: HE/SHE/IT

4 A Find and correct the wrong information in the sentences below. Use the countries in the box to help.

> China   Germany   India
> Japan   ~~Poland~~   Russia   Spain
> the UK   the USA   Turkey

1 Warsaw's in Turkey.
No, it isn't. It's in Poland.
2 Maria Sharapova's from Japan.
3 The Blue Mosque's in Argentina.
4 Heidi Klum's from China.
5 The Great Wall's in Spain.
6 Tokyo's in Italy.
7 Rafael Nadal's from Colombia.
8 The Taj Mahal's in Mexico.
9 Brad Pitt's from Libya.
10 J. K. Rowling's from Russia.

B Work in pairs. Write three false sentences – one about a man, one about a woman, and one about a place.

C Work with other students and take turns. Student A: say a sentence. Other students: say the correct information.

A: Ramires is from the UK.
B: No, he isn't. He's from Brazil.

V THE ALPHABET

5 A Correct the spelling.

1 fone _phone_
2 televison _____
3 camra _____
4 univercity _____
5 resterant _____
6 emial _____
7 futbal _____
8 choklat _____
9 infomashion _____
10 intenet _____

B Work in pairs and take turns. Ask and answer about the spelling.

A: How do you spell 'phone'?
B: p-h-o-n-e.
A: Right.

F GIVING PERSONAL INFORMATION

6 A Look at the business card and write questions for 1–5.

Dr ¹Hakan ²Osman

Bilkent University, Ankara, ³Turkey.
⁴**Phone:** 039 387 4425
⁵**Email:** Osman@mail.bilkent.edu.tr

1 What's your first name?

B Change three things in 1–5 above.

Phone: 034 387 4425

C Work in pairs and take turns. Student A: ask questions 1–5. Student B: answer the questions. Student A: find the three changes.

2 people

SPEAKING 2.1 Talk about photos of family and friends 2.2 Check information about people 2.3 Suggest things to do 2.4 Talk about five people in your life

LISTENING 2.1 Listen to someone talk about photos 2.4 Watch a BBC programme about a royal wedding

READING 2.2 Read about family businesses

WRITING 2.1 Learn to use contractions 2.4 Describe five people in your life

BBC
INTERVIEWS
◉)) Who is in your family?

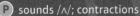

G *be: you/we/they*
P sounds /ʌ/; contractions
V family

A

B

C

D

VOCABULARY

FAMILY

1 A Match people 1–5 with photos A–D.

1 husband and wife   **4** mother and daughter
2 brother and sisters **5** parents and children
3 father and son

B ▶ 2.1 SOUNDS /ʌ/ Listen and underline four words with the sound /ʌ/ as in b<u>u</u>s. Then listen and repeat.

h<u>u</u>sband

C Work in pairs and look at the family tree. Complete 1–9 below.

I am Emma.

1 Suzy is my ___*sister*___.
2 Will is my _____.
3 Tom is my _____.
4 Julia is my _____.
5 Tom and Julia are my _____.

I am Tom.

6 Julia is my _____.
7 Emma and Suzy are my _____.
8 Will is my _____.
9 Emma, Suzy and Will are my _____.

Tom   Julia

Emma   Suzy   Will

D Work in pairs and take turns. Student A: say two names. Student B: say who it is.

A: Julia and Suzy
B: mother and daughter

LISTENING

2 A ▶ 2.2 Listen to three conversations. Which three photos are they talking about?

1 _____   **2** _____   **3** _____

B Listen again and underline the correct alternative.

1 Johnny's *3/4/5*, Amy's *5/6/7* and Jennifer's *8/9/10*.
2 *Jennifer/Amy*'s a musician.
3 *Johnny/Amy*'s on the football team.
4 *Lucy/Tim* 's British.
5 *Lucy/Tim* is American.
6 *She/He*'s a hotel manager.

GRAMMAR

BE: YOU/WE/THEY

3 A Underline the verb *be* in the sentences.

1 **A:** Where <u>are</u> you?
  B: We're in the park.
2 **A:** Are they at the same school?
  B: No, they aren't.
3 **A:** You aren't British.
  B: No, I'm from the US.

B Complete the tables below with the words in the box.

're   Are   aren't   are (x2)

You We They	are _'re_	from China. students. American.
You We They	are not	British. _____ from the US.

_____	you/we/they	good students?
Yes,	you/we/they	_____.
No,		aren't.
Where	_____	you from?

C ▶ 2.3 CONTRACTIONS Listen to the pronunciation of *you're, we're, they're*. Then listen and repeat.

D ▶ 2.4 Listen and write the sentences in your notebook. Then listen and repeat.

▷ page 120 **LANGUAGEBANK**

4 A Underline the correct alternative.

A: This is a photo of Dan.
B: ¹*Is he/Are you* brothers?
A: No, ²*I'm not/we aren't*. ³*He's/We're* good friends.
B: And this photo? ⁴*Are they/Is she* your sisters?
A: No, they ⁵*isn't/aren't*. This is my wife, Maria, with Tina. Tina and Maria are sisters. The photo is in Peru.
B: Are ⁶*they/she* from Peru?
A: No, they ⁷*not/aren't*. ⁸*They're/She's* from Uruguay.
B: ⁹*Is/Are* your wife a teacher?
A: Yes. She and Tina ¹⁰*is/are* teachers.

B ▶ 2.5 Listen and check.

C Work in pairs and practise the conversation.

WRITING

CONTRACTIONS

5 A Look at the example. Complete the contractions for sentences 2–4.

1 They are my parents. *They're my parents.*
2 She is my daughter.
3 We are not sisters.
4 Tom is my brother.

B Underline the correct alternative to complete the rules.

> **RULES**
> 1 *Use/Don't use* contractions in spoken English.
> 2 *Use/Don't use* contractions in text messages and emails to friends.

C Rewrite the text messages using eight contractions.

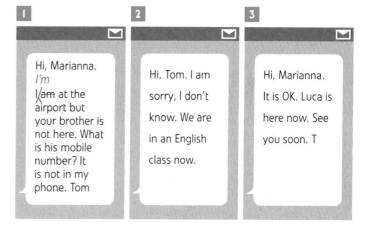

1 Hi, Marianna. I'm I am at the airport but your brother is not here. What is his mobile number? It is not in my phone. Tom

2 Hi, Tom. I am sorry, I don't know. We are in an English class now.

3 Hi, Marianna. It is OK. Luca is here now. See you soon. T

D Work in pairs and take turns. Read out the text messages with the contractions.

SPEAKING

6 A Use two photos of your family or friends and complete the notes below.

Photo 1

Name:
Family or friend:
Nationality:
Job:
Where is he or she now?

B Work with other students. Cover your notes and talk about the photos.

This is my brother, Juan. He's South African. He's an office worker in Cape Town.

7 Work in pairs. Student A: look at the photos on page 148. Student B: look at the photos on page 150.

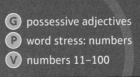

(G) possessive adjectives
(P) word stress: numbers
(V) numbers 11–100

VOCABULARY

NUMBERS 11–100

1 A Write the numbers next to the words.

11 12 13 14 15 16 17 18 19 20

eleven	_11_	twelve	_____	sixteen	_____
nineteen	_____	fifteen	_____	eighteen	_____
twenty	_____	fourteen	_____	seventeen	_____
thirteen	_____				

B ▶ 2.6 Listen and repeat the numbers in order.

C Work in pairs and take turns. Student A: write a number. Student B: say the number.

2 A Complete the numbers.

30	thirty	60	sixty	90	_____
40	forty	70	_____	100	a hundred
50	fifty	80	_____		

B ▶ 2.7 Listen and check. Then listen and repeat.

C ▶ 2.8 **WORD STRESS: numbers** Listen and underline the stressed syllable. Then listen and repeat.

forty fourteen   seventy seventeen
fifty fifteen   eighty eighteen
sixty sixteen   ninety nineteen

D Work in pairs and take turns. Student A: say a number from Exercise 2C. Student B: point to the number.

E ▶ 2.9 Listen and write the numbers.   *1 67*

3 A Write the names and ages of four friends or people in your family.

Eloise 53   Andreas 28

B Work in pairs and take turns. Student A: tell Student B about the people in Exercise 3A. Student B: write down the names and ages.

A: *Eloise is my mother.*
B: *How old is she?*
A: *She's fifty-three.*
B: *How do you spell Eloise?*

READING

4 A Work in pairs and look at the photos. What is the relationship between the people (e.g. husband and wife)?

B Read the text and check your ideas.

C Read the texts again and complete the information.

	Business	Where?	Good things
1	restaurant		small,
2			
3			

Donati's Pizza Place is in downtown Washington, D.C. in the USA. The restaurant manager is Antonio Donati. His sons, Marco and Fabio, are pizza chefs and their friend Leonardo is a waiter. 'Our restaurant is ten years old. It's a real family business. It's small and friendly and the food is great. Come and visit. It's the perfect place for your pizza.'

Star Supermarket is in the centre of Bath, England, and its doors are open 24/7*. Sixty-year-old manager, Alex, is from Jamaica. His wife, Dana, and daughters, Sakina and Mia, and their husbands are the shop assistants. 'Our shop is a family business,' says Dana. 'We're open 24/7 because people shop 24/7.'

*24/7: twenty-four hours a day, seven days a week

GRAMMAR

POSSESSIVE ADJECTIVES

5 A Complete the sentences with *my, your, his, her, its, our, their*. Then check your answers in the texts in Exercise 4A.

1 The restaurant manager is Antonio Donati. ___His___ sons, Marco and Fabio, are pizza chefs and _____ friend Leonardo is a waiter.
2 'Come and visit. It's the perfect place for _____ pizza.'
3 She says, 'It's a real family business. _____ father is here from four o'clock in the morning.'
4 _____ husband isn't in the family business.
5 Star Supermarket is in the centre of Bath, England, and _____ doors are open 24/7.
6 '_____ shop is a family business,' says Dana.

B Complete the table. Use the sentences in Exercise 5A to help.

subject pronoun	possessive adjective
I	my
you	_____
_____	his
she	_____
it	_____
_____	our
they	_____

▷ page 120 **LANGUAGE**BANK

6 A Underline the correct alternative.

The family business is in Spain and the manager is a woman. [1]*His/Her* name is Cristina. [2]*His/Her* husband David is the receptionist and chef. David isn't happy in [3]*his/my* job. [4]*Our/Their* business is in a very beautiful place near a beach. Cristina says, '[5]*Our/Its* name is 'La Perla'. Come and visit. It's a great place for [6]*their/your* holiday. [7]*Our/Their* rooms are very good'. David says, 'Yes, but [8]*my/our* job isn't good!'

B Work in pairs. What is the business in Exercise 6A?

7 Complete the sentences with the words in the box.

~~my~~ his her its our their

Mama's salsa – from mother of three, Lucia Covas Garcia
'The salsa recipe is from [1] ___my___ mother, and [2]_____ name is *Mama's Salsa*. It's a hundred years old,' says Lucia. [3]_____ husband Manolo and [4]_____ son Pablo are all in the family business. Lucia says, 'Pablo and [5]_____ wife, Sonja are the cooks and [6]_____ salsa is on sale all over South America.'

Blue Fish is a fish shop in Sydney, Australia. Young-sun Park is the manager. She says, 'It's a real family business. My father is here from four o'clock in the morning. My son and daughter are at university but they're here in the shop in the evening.' Her husband isn't in the family business. He's a chef in a restaurant, a fish restaurant! 'We really love fish and our fish is the best in the city,' says Young-sun.

SPEAKING

8 Work in pairs. Student A: turn to page 148. Student B: turn to page 150.

F making suggestions
P intonation: showing interest
V feelings

VOCABULARY

FEELINGS

1 A Match the adjectives in the box with pictures A–F.

> hot *A*   cold   hungry   thirsty   tired   bored

B ▶ 2.10 Listen and check your answers. Then listen and repeat.

C Work in pairs and take turns. Student A: ask about a problem and point to a picture. Student B: say the problem.

A: What's the problem?
B: He's tired.

D Work in pairs and ask about your feelings. Find three things in common.

A: Are you hot?
B: No, I'm not. Are you?
A: Yes, I am.

▷ page 140 **PHOTOBANK**

A

FUNCTION

MAKING SUGGESTIONS

2 A Which verbs in the box are in the photos?

> eat   have a coffee/drink   have a break   sit down
> go   stop

B ▶ 2.11 Listen and match conversations 1–3 with photos A–C.

1 _____   2 _____   3 _____

C Listen again. Are the sentences true (T) or false (F)?

1 **a)** They're at university. *T*
   b) Café Lugo is a Spanish cafe.
2 **a)** It isn't their first meeting.
   b) His first name's Lee.
3 **a)** They're tired and hot.
   b) They're hungry.

D Correct the false sentences.

3 A Listen again and complete the conversations with a verb from Exercise 2A. Do <u>not</u> use one of the verbs.

1 **A:** I'm hungry.
   B: Yeah, me, too. Let's ____*eat*____ something.
2 **A:** OK, Lena. And I'm Ken.
   B: Let's _____. Coffee?
   A: Yes, please.
3 **A:** Let's _____.
   B: Good idea. I'm tired.
4 **A:** Let's _____.
   B: Yeah, OK. Let's _____.

B Complete the rule.

> **RULES**
>
> Use _____ + verb to make a suggestion.

C ▶ 2.12 Listen and underline the stressed words in Exercise 3A. Then listen and repeat.

Let's <u>eat</u> something.

▷ page 120 **LANGUAGEBANK**

4

A Complete the conversations with the words in the box.

| 'm problem Me too break 's a Let |

1 **A:** I ¹ ____'m____ bored.
   B: Me, ² _____.
   A: ³ _____ 's stop now.
   B: Good idea.
2 **A:** What's the ⁴ _____ ?
   B: I'm cold.
   A: Me, too. Let ⁵ _____ go inside.
   B: OK.
   A: OK, let's have a ⁶ _____ for fifteen minutes.
3 **B:** I'm thirsty.
   A: ⁷ _____ too.
   B: Let's have ⁸ _____ coffee.

B Work in pairs and practise the conversations.

LEARN TO

RESPOND TO SUGGESTIONS

5 A ▶ 2.13 **INTONATION: showing interest** Listen to the answers. Are they interested (+) or not interested (–)? Tick + or – .

1   ✓   4

2   5 ⊕ ⊖

3 ⊕ ⊖   6 ⊕ ⊖

speakout TIP

Use intonation to show you are interested or happy.

Great!

B Work in pairs and take turns. Student A: say *Great/OK/Good idea*. Student B: point to + or –.

SPEAKING

6 A Work in pairs and complete the conversation for Student A. Add the missing words.

Student A

| I / hungry. |
| *I'm hungry.* |

                                                    Student B

                              | Me too. |

| Let / eat. |
| _____ |

                              | OK. Where? |

| Let / go / to (name of café) |
| _____ |

                              | Good idea. |

B Work in pairs and practise the conversation.

C Cover the conversation and practise it again.

7

Work with other students. Start your conversation with the adjectives in the box. Make suggestions for places to go.

| tired hungry hot thirsty cold bored |

A: *I'm tired.*
B: *Me too.*
A: *Let's go and have a coffee.*
B: *Good idea. Where?*
A: *Let's go to …*

Kate Middleton

Prince William

Prince Harry

Prince Charles

Elton John

David and Victoria Beckham

Pippa Middleton

Queen Elizabeth and Prince Phillip

DVD PREVIEW

1 A Work in pairs and look at the photos of people. What is their relationship to William and Kate?

A: *Prince Harry is his brother.*
B: *Yes, and I think Prince Charles is his …*

B Read the programme information. Who is at the royal wedding? Where is it?

◗)) The Royal Wedding: William and Catherine

BBC

Thousands of people are in the streets of London and billions of people around the world are by their TVs, all for the royal wedding of Prince William and Kate Middleton. The BBC programme *Royal Wedding* is the story of their big day. Their families and friends are all at Westminster Abbey for the wedding.

DVD VIEW

2 A Watch the DVD and number the people in the photos in the order you see them.

David and Victoria Beckham 1

B Match the underlined words in sentences 1–6 with people a)–f).

1 <u>They're</u> in the streets of London. c
2 <u>They're</u> friends of Prince William.
3 <u>He's</u> in the car with Kate.
4 <u>They</u> arrive with Pippa Middleton.
5 In the Royal Family, <u>they</u> arrive first.
6 <u>She</u> meets Kate at the car.

a) children
b) her father
c) people
d) Pippa Middleton
e) Prince William and Prince Harry
f) the Beckhams

C Watch the DVD again to check your answers.

D Correct one word in each sentence. Then watch the DVD again to check your answers.

                 wedding
1 Today is the ~~birthday~~ of Prince William and Kate Middleton.
2 Victoria and David Beckham, friends of Prince William, are hungry.
3 The rich and famous are here including the actor, Elton John …
4 Her sister, Pippa Middleton, arrives with children of friends and fathers.
5 The big moment … and a woman with the ring.
6 The end of a big holiday for Kate and William.

speakout five people in your life

3 A ▶ 2.14 Listen to Jo talk about five people in her life. Match the names with people 1–5.

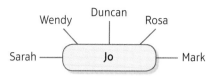

Wendy   Duncan   Rosa

Sarah — Jo — Mark

1 a person in her family *Duncan*   4 her teacher
2 a student in her class   5 a person at her work
3 a good friend

B Listen again and tick the key phrases you hear.

> **KEY PHRASES**
>
> OK, five people in my life. The first is [name].
> Duncan's [my brother/a very good friend/my manager/…].
> Who is [she/he/Mark/…]?
> [She/He's] very nice, very friendly.
> Wendy is [my sister/a student/a friend from work/…].
> We're in a Spanish class together.
> We're friends.

C Write the names of five people in your life. Write two things about each person on another page.

Talya – a friend from university, an actress
Emir – my brother, twenty-six

D Work in pairs and take turns. Student A: show your partner the names of your five people and talk about them. Student B: ask questions.

A: Talya's a friend from university. She's an actress.
B: How old is she?
A: She's …
B: Is she a good friend?

writeback a description

4 A Read the information and answer the questions.

1 Who is in her family?
2 Who isn't a friend?
3 Who is her best friend?

My name is Melis. I'm twenty-nine. I'm Turkish and I'm a doctor in Izmir. There are five important people in my life:

Talya is my best friend from university. She's twenty-eight and she's from Ankara. She's an actress.

Emir is my brother. He's twenty-six, and he's a teacher.

Ali is my mother. We're on the phone a lot!

Poppy's a friend from work. She's a nurse from the UK. She's married to a Turkish businessman. She's a very happy person.

Pasqualo isn't a friend, but he's a nice person. He's from Italy. He's a waiter at a restaurant in my city.

B Write descriptions of your five people from Exercise 3C. Write 60–100 words.

Ⓥ FAMILY

1 A Look at the diagram. Write the names of the people.

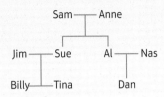

Sam —— Anne

Jim —— Sue   Al —— Nas

Billy —— Tina   Dan

1 My father is Sam and my sister is Sue. *Al*

2 My daughter is Tina and my wife is Sue.

3 My mother is Sue and my sister is Tina.

4 My parents are Sam and Anne and my brother is Al.

5 My son is Dan and my husband is Al.

6 My children are Sue and Al and my husband is Sam.

B Write three more sentences about the people in the diagram.

1 My brother is …

C Work in pairs and take turns. Student A: read out a sentence. Student B: say the name.

Ⓖ BE: YOU/WE/THEY

2 A Complete the conversation with the words in the box.

> are (x4)   is (x2)   they (x3)
> we   're

A: Who ¹ __are__ they?

B: ² _____ 're my friends Ali and Hesna.

A: Where ³ _____ ⁴ _____ from?

B: ⁵ _____ ⁶ _____ from Syria.

A: ⁷ _____ you friends from school?

B: No, ⁸ _____ 're friends from university.

A: ⁹ _____ they married?

B: Ali ¹⁰ _____ n't married. Hesna ¹¹ _____ married to my brother.

B Write the names of two of your friends.

C Work in pairs and take turns. Ask and answer questions about the friends.

A: Who are they?
B: They're Yumiko and Kenji.

Ⓥ NUMBERS 11–100

3 A Write the numbers in words.

1 twenty-one + (plus) nine = ___*thirty*___

2 ninety-nine – (minus) eleven = _____

3 eighty-three + fourteen = _____

4 thirty-two – five = _____

B Complete the questions with a number.

1 What's 62 – ____?

2 What's 15 + ____?

3 What's 81 – ____?

4 What's 19 + ____?

C Work in pairs and take turns. Ask and answer the questions.

Ⓖ POSSESSIVE ADJECTIVES

4 A Find and correct the mistakes.

1 I'm Chinese and I'm name's Jun.

2 You're in Room 108 and Mr Watts is you're teacher.

3 He's John. He's surname's Wayford.

4 She's name's Vera and she's a singer.

5 We're students and we're class is Room Ten.

6 They're names are Ahmed and Ali and they're from Egypt.

B Complete the sentences about yourself and other students. Write five true sentences and one false sentence.

1 I'm _____ and my _____ is _____.

2 You're _____ and your _____ is _____.

3 _____ 's from _____ and his _____ is _____.

4 _____ 's from _____ and her _____ is _____.

5 We're _____ and our _____ is _____.

6 They're _____ and their _____ is _____.

I'm Veronika and my surname's Cruz.
She's from Italy and her name's Louisa.

C Work in pairs and take turns. Student A: read your sentences. Student B: which sentence is false?

A: We're students and our teacher's Keira.
B: False! Our teacher's Natalie.

Ⓥ FEELINGS

5 A Add the vowels to complete the feelings.

1 h_o_t

2 h__ngry

3 t__r__d

4 c__ld

5 th__rsty

6 b__r__d

B Work in pairs and take turns. Student A: close your book. Student B: mime a feeling. Student A: say the feeling.

Ⓕ MAKING SUGGESTIONS

6 A Put the words in the correct order to complete the conversation.

A: go / Let's / now.

Let's go now.

B: tired / I'm / No, / Let's / down / sit.

A: a / let's / and / have / stop / OK, / break.

B: Are / thirsty / you?

A: Yes, / am / I.

B: to / go / Let's / café / a.

A: idea / Good.

B Work in pairs. Write one key word from each sentence.

go
tired
sit

C Work in pairs and practise the conversation. Use the key words to help.

READING AND GRAMMAR

1 A Work in pairs and look at pictures A–E. Where are they?

B Read the messages. Write the names next to the letters.

A _Katja_   C _____   E _____

B _____   D _____

---

1 3.10pm | 16/09/16 | Azra

Azra is a singer from Bogotá, Colombia. She's twenty-four years old and sings at festivals all over the world. Her music is a mix of traditional Indian and modern rock. Her concert is tonight at 8p.m. Please come and see her sing!

---

2 4.14pm | 16/09/16 | Katja2411

Hi, everybody! I'm Katja and I'm from Germany. I'm here with my brother, Lukas. He's also German, of course. We're office workers in Berlin. Lukas is a big music fan. It's my first time, and I'm very happy to be here. We're in the Festival Hotel in room 217 – please come and say hello!

---

3 **LOST** Fifi and Bruno, my two dogs. Fifi is black and she's one year old. Bruno is white and he's four. They're very friendly. If Fifi and Bruno are with you, text me (Jasmine) on 443 908 9442.

C Read the messages again. What are the numbers? Write age, room, or phone and the name.

4   _age, Bruno_

217   _____

4439089442 _____

24   _____

1   _____

D What festivals are in your country? Are they good?

---

2 A Complete the questions with words from the box. Do not use one of the words.

are (x 2)   they   how   her   his   is (x 2)   it

1 _Are_ Katja and Lukas from Spain?
2 _____ Lukas a singer?
3 Is Katja _____ sister?
4 Where _____ Azra from?
5 When is _____ concert?
6 _____ Fifi and Bruno cats?
7 Are _____ friendly?
8 _____ old is Bruno?

B Work in pairs and take turns to ask and answer the questions.

A: Are Katja and Lukas from Spain?
B: No, they aren't. They're from Germany.

3 Complete the messages with the correct form of *be*.

I' ¹_m_ here with a group of students from St. Petersburg, and we' ²_____ at the festival for the first time. My room ³_____ in the student hotel. The hotel ⁴_____ (not) very nice, but the hotel workers ⁵_____ all very friendly. ⁶_____ you here alone? Don't be alone – come and see us. Let's have a party!

✉

Arturo, ⁷_____ you here? Where are you? Jeff and I ⁸_____ at the HJ Hotel in room 102. Please come and see us!

Robin

LISTENING

Morelli | Haru | Fatimah | Takahashi | Churchill | Gonzales

4 A Work in pairs and look at the names of people at the festival. What nationality are the people?

B ▶ C1.1 Listen and check.

C Listen again. Who talks about food (F), drink (D), music (M)?

Speaker 1 _____   Speaker 2 _____   Speaker 3 _____

D Work in pairs and write the missing words. Then listen again and check.

1 B: It's good music, yeah?
   A: Yeah, it's _____.

2 B: Is Fatimah your surname or your first name?
   A: It's my _____ name.

3 A: Hey, I'm hungry.
   B: Me too. Let's go and _____ something.

4 A: Your English is very good!
   B: Thanks, but I'm from the _____.
   A: Oh, I'm _____.

SPEAKING

5 Work in pairs. Student A: turn to page 153. Student B: look at the table below. Ask questions to complete the information.

First name	¹Haru	²Fatimah	³Lukas and Katja
Surname		Hassan	
Nationality	Japanese		German
Age		23	
Job	teacher		office workers
Email address			Neil42@tmail.com Kat@px.co.uk

B: Number one is Haru. What's his surname?
A: Nakamura.
B: How do you spell it?
A: N-A-K-A-M-U-R-A. What's his nationality?

6 A Draw five circles on a piece of paper. In the first circle, write the names of three people in your family. In the other four circles, write their ages, jobs, relationship to you and where they are now.

Marcello / Ana / Daniel — teacher / chef / student — 32 / 17 / 55 — brother / grandmother / father — Rome / Venice / Florence

B Work in pairs and take turns. Look at your partner's information. Ask and answer about each person.

A: Is Daniel your brother?
B: Yes, he is.
A: Is he a teacher?

SOUNDS: /æ/ AND /ə/

7 A ▶ C1.2 Listen to the sounds. Then listen and repeat.

/æ/	/ə/
taxi	teacher

B ▶ R1.3 Listen and put the words in the box in the correct group. Then listen and repeat.

~~doctor~~ ~~actor~~ England
nationality computer
understand happy daughter

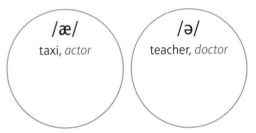

/æ/	/ə/
taxi, *actor*	teacher, *doctor*

8 A Work in groups. Complete the words and circle the sound in each word.

	/ə/
a country	J@pan
son and daughter	ch_____
a number	se_____
www	in_____
TV	te_____
a country	In_____

	/æ/
it's for photos	c@mera
mother, father, son and daughter	fa_____
woman in a film	ac_____
money place	ba_____
big letters	ca_____
a job	ma_____

B Work with other students and compare your answers.

3 things

WHAT'S THIS? p30

FAMOUS CLOTHES p32

A COFFEE, PLEASE p34

THE MARKET p36

SPEAKING **3.1** Ask about objects **3.2** Talk about possessions **3.3** Order food and drink **3.4** Buy things in a market

LISTENING **3.1** Listen to conversations between students **3.3** Listen to people in a café **3.4** Watch a BBC programme about a famous market

READING **3.2** Read descriptions of famous clothes from films **3.3** Read about some famous cafés

WRITING **3.2** Use linkers *and, but* **3.4** Write about a market

BBC
INTERVIEWS

What are your favourite things?

3.1))) WHAT'S THIS?

G this/that/these/those
P sounds: plurals /s/ /z/ and /ɪz/
V things

A

Hi Tanya. What are those books?

Hi Denise. These books? _____.

B

Hey Leyla, what's that?

_____.

VOCABULARY

THINGS

1 A Work in pairs and look at photos A–D. Which objects in the box are in the photos?

> books   a tablet computer   keys   a notebook
> cups   boxes   a chair   a table   pens   glasses

B Which words in the box are singular and which are plurals? Write *S* or *Pl*.

C ▶ 3.1   SOUNDS: plurals /s/ /z/ and /ɪz/   Look at the pronunciation of the plural words. Then listen and repeat.

/s/ book<u>s</u>   cup<u>s</u>
/z/ key<u>s</u>   pen<u>s</u>
/ɪz/ box<u>es</u>   glass<u>es</u>

▷ page 140 **PHOTOBANK**

LISTENING

2 A ▶ 3.2   Listen and match conversations 1–4 with photos A–D.

1 _____   2 _____   3 _____   4 _____

B Listen again. Who is <u>not</u> happy? Circle four names.

> Denise   Tanya   Stan   Nasrin   Leyla   Sam
> Oliver   Kate   Dave

C Work in pairs and look at photos A–D. Complete the conversations with 1–4 below.

1 Yeah, this one's very heavy.
2 It's our homework.
3 They're for my English class.
4 This one?

GRAMMAR

THIS/THAT/THESE/THOSE

3 A Circle *this*, *that*, *these*, *those* in the conversations in photos A–D.

B Write *this*, *that*, *these*, *those* under pictures 1–4.

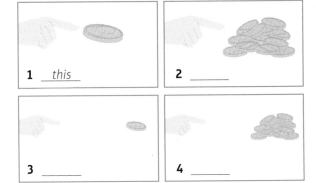

1 ___this___   2 _____

3 _____   4 _____

C Complete the rule with *is* or *are*.

> **RULES**
> 1 Use *these/those* + _____.
> 2 Use *this/that* + _____.

D ▶ 3.3   Listen and number the words in the order you hear them. Then listen again and repeat.

1 __2__ this __1__ that
2 _____ this _____ that
3 _____ these _____ those
4 _____ these _____ those
5 _____ this _____ these
6 _____ this _____ these

▷ page 122 **LANGUAGEBANK**

Sam, is that my coffee?

_____.

Yes.

Hey, Kate, what's in these boxes?

My cups are in that box. My glasses are in this one.

_____.

4 A Celine is a new student in a language school. Complete the conversation with *this, that, these* or *those*.

A: Celine, ¹ _this_ is the students' room and ² _____ are my friends over there.

B: Where are they from?

A: They're from Greece and Brazil. Hi, everyone. ³ _____ is Celine, from France.

B: Hello.

A: OK, Celine. Here's our classroom and ⁴ _____ is our teacher over there, Mrs King. Mrs King!

C: Yes. Who's ⁵ _____? Oh hello, Sylvie. And you're the new student, yes?

B: Yes, I'm Celine. Hello.

C: Hello, Celine. Welcome to the class. ⁶ _____ is your coursebook.

B: Thank you.

C: And have one of ⁷ _____ dictionaries here.

B: Thanks.

C: Please sit down. ⁸ _____ desk is free, over there by the window.

B Work in groups and practise the conversation.

speakout TIP

Introduce people with *This is* + name: *This is my sister, Tina. This is Dr Meyer.*
Mr = man; *Ms* = married or single woman; *Mrs* = married woman; *Miss* = single woman; *Dr* = Doctor

SPEAKING

5 A Work in pairs. Choose three things in the classroom and three things from your bag.

B Write the English words for the things. Look in a dictionary or ask your teacher.

C Work in groups and take turns. Point to your objects and ask questions.

A: *What are those in English?*
B: *They're keys. What's this in English?*
C: *I don't know.*
D: *It's a purse.*

6 Work in pairs and take turns. Student A: you are a new student. Student B: you are an old student. Show Student A around the classroom. Show the places and things in the classroom, and introduce Student A to other students.

3.2))) FAMOUS CLOTHES

G possessive 's
P sounds: possessive 's
V colours and clothes

VOCABULARY

COLOURS AND CLOTHES

1 A Write the colours and clothes from the boxes under the pictures below.

colours

black   white   ~~brown~~   green   red   blue

clothes

a hat   jeans   a shirt   a jacket   a sweater   ~~shoes~~

1 _brown shoes_   2 _____

3 _____   4 _____

5 _____   6 _____

B ▶ 3.4 Listen and check. Then listen again and repeat.

C Work in pairs and sit back to back. Take turns to describe your partner's clothes.

A: Your shoes are brown.
B: No they aren't, they're white.

▷ page 141 **PHOTOBANK**

2 A Complete the conversation in two different ways with words from the box.

~~ring~~   shoes   great   Spain   good   on you   my girlfriend

A: Nice ¹ _ring_ !/² _____ !
B: Thanks. It's/They're from ³ _____ ./⁴ _____ .
A: It's/They're ⁵ _____ ./⁶ _____ .
B: Thanks.

B Work with other students and practise the conversation about their clothes or other possessions.

A: Nice ring!
B: Thanks. It's …

READING

3 A Look at the photos of films 1–6. Who are the film characters?

B Match the clothes a)–f) to the film characters 1–6.

C Read the article and check your ideas.

D Read the article again and find:

one nationality	two red things
one city	two jobs
two names of films	five names of people in films

4 A Work in pairs. Write two famous things or clothes from films.

B Work in groups. What are the best things or clothes for the exhibition?

A: A black umbrella from Mary Poppins.
B: That's a good idea.
C: I don't know that film.

IN THE FILMS

'In the Films' is a great new exhibition for cinema fans – an exhibition of famous clothes from films. So, what are the top six?

6 'This is Sherlock's hat,' says Kim Clark from the National Film Museum. 'British detective Sherlock Holmes is world-famous but his hat isn't in the books, only in the films.'

5 'Dorothy's shoes from *The Wizard of Oz*. They're a beautiful red colour,' says Kim. 'I really love red.'

4 'These are Mr Bean's brown jacket and red tie,' says Kim. 'His YouTube video from the London Olympics is famous around the world.'

3 'Harry Potter's glasses from the famous children's films. The boy wizard's glasses are in all eight films.'

2 'Is this James Bond's jacket?' I ask. 'Yes, it's James Bond's evening jacket,' Kim says. 'But in this photo of actor Daniel Craig as James Bond, his dinner jacket is black.'

SO WHAT'S NUMBER ONE?

'It's this gold ring' says Kim, 'Frodo's ring from *The Lord of the Rings*. It's the most famous ring in the world.'

a)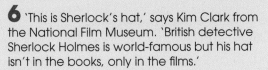

b)

c)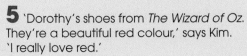

d)

e)

f)

GRAMMAR

POSSESSIVE *'S*

5 A Add *'s* in the correct place in each sentence. Use the text to help.

1 This is Sherlock ˢhat.
2 'These are Mr Bean brown jacket and red tie.'
3 'Is this James Bond jacket?' I ask.
4 At number five are Dorothy shoes from *The Wizard of Oz*.

B Complete the rule.

RULES	Use a name + _____ for the possessive.

6 A Add words to make the questions and answers.

1 these / Nico / books? Yes / they.
Are these Nico's books? Yes, they are.
2 that / Yasmin / bag? Yes / it.
3 those / James / books? No / they.
4 this / Kate / phone? No / it.

B ▶ 3.5 SOUNDS: possessive *'s*
Listen and check. Then listen again and match the names in 1–4 with the sounds.
/s/
/z/ *Nico's*
/ɪz/

C Change questions 1–4 to make questions about students and things in your classroom.

1 Are those Julio's books?

D Work in pairs and take turns. Ask and answer the questions.

▷ page 122 **LANGUAGEBANK**

WRITING

LINKERS *AND, BUT*

7 A Complete the sentences with *and* or *but* .

1 My favourite colour is blue _____ I really love this red T-shirt.
2 My favourite colour is blue _____ my favourite film is *The Lord of the Rings*.

B Choose the correct endings of the sentences.

1 It's a big gold ring with writing around it but
   a) it's the most famous ring in the world.
   b) the writing isn't in English.
2 Sherlock's hat is in all the films and
   a) it isn't in the books.
   b) it's a traditional hat from the countryside.
3 In the exhibition the jacket's white but
   a) in the photo it's black.
   b) it's from an old James Bond film.
4 One pair of these shoes is in a Hollywood museum and
   a) their price is two to three million dollars.
   b) Dorothy's dress is not in the museum.

C Add *and* (x3) and *but* (x3) to the information.

My name's Yves. It's a French name ᵇᵘᵗ I'm not French, I'm Canadian. My parents are teachers I'm not a teacher. I'm a hotel manager my wife's the chef in our hotel. She's from Argentina her name's Natalia. She's a great chef at home I'm the cook! Our son's name is Tomas he's nine years old.

D Write about yourself and your family. Use *and* and *but*. Write 50–70 words.

SPEAKING

8 Work in pairs. Student A: turn to page 149. Student B: turn to page 151.

F ordering in a café
P intonation: phrases with *or*
V food and drink

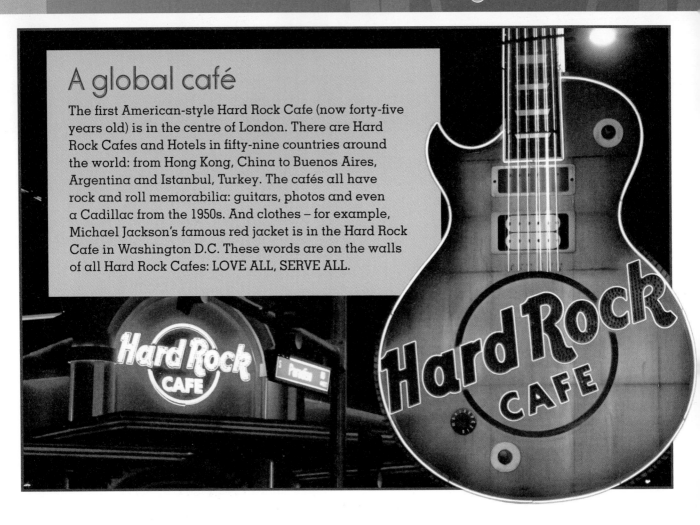

A global café

The first American-style Hard Rock Cafe (now forty-five years old) is in the centre of London. There are Hard Rock Cafes and Hotels in fifty-nine countries around the world: from Hong Kong, China to Buenos Aires, Argentina and Istanbul, Turkey. The cafés all have rock and roll memorabilia: guitars, photos and even a Cadillac from the 1950s. And clothes – for example, Michael Jackson's famous red jacket is in the Hard Rock Cafe in Washington D.C. These words are on the walls of all Hard Rock Cafes: LOVE ALL, SERVE ALL.

VOCABULARY

FOOD AND DRINK

1 A Look at the photo. Is there a Hard Rock Cafe in your town? What other countries is it in?

B Read the information. Are the sentences true (T) or false (F)?

1 The first Hard Rock Cafe is in the USA.
2 Hard Rock Cafes are in a lot of different countries.
3 The cafés all have rock and roll singers.
4 The jacket in one Hard Rock Cafe is Michael Jackson's.
5 Hard Rock Cafes all have one thing in common.

C Work in pairs and answer the questions.

1 What's your favourite type of café or restaurant, e.g. Chinese, Indian, pizza?
2 What cafés or restaurants are good near you?
3 What's your favourite food and drink in a café?

2 A Match phrases 1–6 with pictures A–F.

1 A sandwich and a coffee

2 A tea and a cake

3 A mineral water and a sandwich

4 A cola and a cake

5 A tea and a mineral water

6 A coffee and a cola

B Work in pairs and check your answers.

C Work in pairs and cover the words in 1–6 above. Take turns to order the food and drink.

A: Can I help you?
B: A sandwich and a coffee, please.
A: OK, here you are.

FUNCTION

ORDERING IN A CAFÉ

3 A ▶ 3.6 Listen to the conversations and correct the customers' orders.

1 one white coffee with sugar
2 two espresso coffees and one cappuccino
3 one egg sandwich (white bread), one chocolate cake, one cola
4 one sparkling mineral water, one sandwich

B Who says the sentences? Write C (customer) or W (waiter).

a) How much is that? *C*
b) Anything else?
c) Still or sparkling?
d) Can I have a mineral water, please?
e) No, thank you.
f) That's three euros.
g) Sparkling, please.

C ▶ 3.7 Number sentences a)–g) in order. Then listen and check.

4 A Complete the table.

_____ I have	a	mineral water, please?
	two	coffees, _____?
Still	_____	sparkling?
Espresso		cappuccino?
		Sparkling, please.
		Espresso, please.

B ▶ 3.8 INTONATION: phrases with *or* Listen and tick the intonation you hear. Then listen again and repeat.

1 Still or sparkling?   2 Still or sparkling?

C Work in pairs and take turns. Ask and answer using the words in the box.

Coffee / tea?   Espresso / cappuccino?   Still / sparkling?

A: Coffee or tea?
B: Can I have a tea, please?

5 A Work in pairs. Add words to make a conversation.

Student A

have / coffee, please?
Can I have a coffee, please?

Student B

espresso / cappuccino?
Espresso or cappuccino?

cappuccino

Anything else?

have / mineral water, please?

still / sparkling?

sparkling

OK / five euros

B Work in pairs and take turns. Practise the conversation.

▷ page 122 **LANGUAGEBANK**

LEARN TO

SAY PRICES

6 A ▶ 3.9 Listen and number the prices in order.

| 3.00 | 2.50 | 10 | 1.50 *1* | 5.20 | 12.75 |

B Listen again and repeat.

C ▶ 3.10 Listen to the conversations and write the prices.

speakout TIP

Say prices with the name (e.g. euros) or with no name: 3.99 = *three euros ninety-nine* OR *three ninety-nine*.

D Write four things and four prices.
newspaper – 1.25

E Work in pairs and take turns. Student A: read the things and the prices. Student B: write the things and the prices.

SPEAKING

7 Work in pairs. Student A: turn to page 148. Student B: turn to page 153. Then change roles.

DVD PREVIEW

1 A Match objects 1–6 with pictures A–F.

1 spices *D*		**4** jewellery	
2 clothes		**5** pottery	
3 carpets		**6** leather wallets and bags	

B Which objects in Exercise 1A are in markets in your town or city?

2 Read the programme information. Where is Francesco? What is his new job?

◑)) Francesco's Mediterranean Voyage

BBC

Francesco da Mosto is an Italian TV presenter. In this programme Francesco is in Istanbul, Turkey, at the Grand Bazaar – Istanbul's famous market. His new 'job' is a carpet seller but he says 'I don't know anything about carpets!' His friend and teacher, Harkan, helps him. Is Francesco a good salesman?

DVD VIEW

3 A Watch the DVD. Which objects in Exercise 1A are in the market? Tick the objects.

B Watch the DVD again and underline the word you hear in the sentences.

1 My *first/second* day in Istanbul.
2 There are four *hundred/thousand* shops here.
3 I'm here to *study/learn*.
4 This is *new/nice*. This looks old but it is not old.
5 This is a *free/real* art. Like Turkish Picasso.
6 It's *not good/a nightmare*!
7 **A:** Three hundred dollars.
   B: *Eight/Nine* hundred.
8 Americans are good. They are *friendly/beautiful*.
9 It's his first *carpet/sale*.
10 We will give you a special *discount/price*, five hundred dollars.

C Work in pairs and answer the questions.

1 Is Francesco a good salesman?
2 Is Harkan (the Turkish man) a good salesman?

speakout in a market

4 A ▶ 3.11 Listen to the conversation. Are the sentences true (T) or false (F)? Correct the false sentences.

1 The lamps are from Morocco. *F They're from Turkey.*
2 The seller's first price is 215.
3 The woman's first price is 50.
4 The final price is 150.

B Listen again and tick the key phrases you hear.

> **KEY PHRASES**
>
> Excuse me.
> Where is [this/that] [lamp/carpet] from?
> Where are [these/those] [lamps/carpets] from?
> Can I have a look?
> This one?
> No, that one.
> How much [is it/are they]?
> That's expensive.
> For you, a special [discount/price].

C Work in pairs and take turns. Student A: you are the customer. Choose an item from Exercise 1A. Student B: you are the seller. Choose a price. Role-play the situation.

A: *Excuse me.*
B: *Yes.*
A: *Where is that lamp from?*
B: *This one?*
A: *No, that one.*

writeback a description

5 A Read the description of a market and answer the questions.

1 What's the name of the market?
2 Where is it?
3 Is it open every day?
4 What is it good for?

Covent Garden market is in the centre of London. It's open every day and it's good for beautiful jewellery, clothes and pictures. It's also good for small shops and cafés. It's a famous tourist attraction for visitors to London and there are people from all around the world. I'm not a tourist, I'm from London, but for me Covent Garden market is a good place to stop and have a break.

B Write about a market in your town/city or another town/city. Answer the questions in Exercise 5A. Write 80–100 words.

ⓥ THINGS

1 Add the vowels to complete the objects.

1 b_o__k
2 t__bl__
3 gl__ss__s
4 ch__ __r
5 n__t__b__ __k
6 k__y
7 t__bl__t c__mp__t__r
8 b__x
9 c__p
10 p__n

ⓖ THIS/THAT/ THESE/THOSE

2 A Complete the conversation with *this*, *that*, *these* or *those*.

Jan: Maria, ¹ _this_ is my husband, Carlos. Carlos, ² _____ is my friend from school, Maria.

Carlos: Hello, Maria. Nice to meet you.

Maria: You too. Are ³ _____ your children?

Carlos: Yes, ⁴ _____ is my daughter, Ana, and ⁵ _____ is my son, Paolo.

Maria: Hi.

Carlos: Say *hi* to Maria.

Ana and Paolo: Hi.

Carlos: Is ⁶ _____ your car over there?

Maria: Yes, it is. And ⁷ _____ are my children in the car. Come and say *hi*.

B Work in groups and practise the conversation.

C Work in pairs. Write a new name, nationality and job for your partner.

Naomi, British, hairdresser

D Work in groups. Introduce your partner.

A: Li Wei, this is Naomi. Naomi, this is Li Wei.
B: Hi …

ⓥ COLOURS AND CLOTHES

3 A Put the letters in the correct order to make four clothes and four colours. The first letter is underlined.

1 rewet_s_a
2 kla_b_c
3 l_b_eu
4 thir_s_
5 taje_c_k
6 re_n_ge
7 re_t_sours
8 nor_b_w

B Write three more clothes and three colours.

C Work in pairs and take turns. Student A: say a word and ask about the spelling. Student B: spell it.

A: How do you spell shoes?
B: s-h-o-e-s

ⓖ POSSESSIVE 'S

4 A Complete the captions with a name from the box.

Mozart   Ronaldo   Taylor Swift
Picasso   Serena Williams
Michael Jackson

1 _____ piano
2 _____ guitar
3 _____ brush
4 _____ tennis racquet
5 _____ football
6 _____ glove

B Work in pairs and take turns. Student A: choose a student's possession. Say *It's …* and the name of the person. Student B: ask three questions to find the object.

A: It's Radu's.
B: Is it Radu's pen?
A: No, it isn't.
B: Is it … ?

ⓥ FOOD AND DRINK

5 Find and circle seven food and drink words.

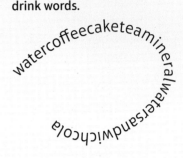

watercoffeecaketeamineralwatersandwichcola

ⓕ ORDERING IN A CAFÉ

6 A Add words to make a conversation.

A: ¹help / you?
Can I help you?
B: ²egg sandwich
A: ³White / brown?
B: ⁴White
A: ⁵else?
B: ⁶mineral water
A: ⁷Still / sparkling?
B: ⁸Sparkling. How much / that?
A: ⁹$6.90
B: ¹⁰here / are

B Work in pairs and practise the conversation. Then cover your answers and practise it again.

7 A Complete the pairs with your ideas.

1 coffee / _tea_
2 cappuccino / _____
3 still / _____
4 euros / _____
5 black / _____
6 pen / _____
7 trousers / _____
8 trainers / _____

B Work in groups. Student A: say one of your words and *or*. The other students: complete the question. Pay attention to the intonation.

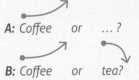

A: Coffee   or   … ?

B: Coffee   or   tea?

4

life

BBC
INTERVIEWS

◁)) What do you do
for fun?

G present simple: *I/you/we/they*
P sentence stress
V verb phrases

VOCABULARY

VERB PHRASES

1 A Complete the word webs with the words and phrases in the box.

> ~~coffee~~   a small car   Exercise 3A   to a restaurant
> in a flat   English   in an office   ~~a phone~~

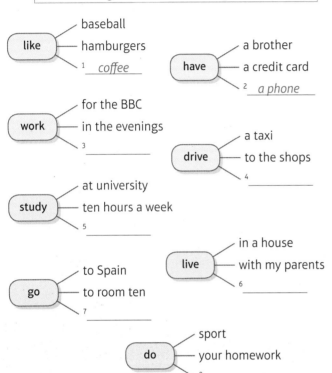

like — baseball
— hamburgers
— 1 *coffee*

have — a brother
— a credit card
— 2 *a phone*

work — for the BBC
— in the evenings
— 3 _____

drive — a taxi
— to the shops
— 4 _____

study — at university
— ten hours a week
— 5 _____

live — in a house
— with my parents
— 6 _____

go — to Spain
— to room ten
— 7 _____

do — sport
— your homework
— 8 _____

B Work in pairs. Which phrases from Exercise 1A are in the photos?

C Work in pairs and add one verb phrase to each verb.

like chocolate

D Work in pairs. Student A: say a verb. Student B: say a word or phrase that goes with it.

A: *Like.*
B: *Like baseball. Go.*
A: *Go to a restaurant.*

E Work in pairs and take turns. Student A: say a sentence about yourself. Student B: say if it's true for you.

A: *I like coffee.*
B: *Me, too. (✓) I work in an office.*
A: *I don't. (✗)*

speakout TIP

It's good to write and learn verb phrases (*work in an office*), not just verbs (*work*). Write five verb phrases with *be* in your phrasebook now.

▷ page 142 **PHOTOBANK**

LISTENING

2 A Read the programme information. Are the people from the USA?

> **11a.m. - The USA today**
> People from different countries speak about their life in the USA and answer this question: Is life in the USA the same or different from other countries?

B ▶ 4.1   Listen and number the topics in the order people talk about them. One topic is <u>not</u> in the listening.

> friends   students   American football
> houses 1   cars

C Listen again and underline the correct alternative.

1 In the USA, people live in *houses/flats.*
2 Students have jobs in the *mornings/evenings.*
3 People *drive/walk* two hundred metres to the shops.
4 My American friends like *the same/different* things.

D Work in pairs and discuss. Which things in 1–3 above are the same or different in your country?

GRAMMAR

PRESENT SIMPLE: *I/YOU/WE/THEY*

3 A Underline the verbs in the sentences.

1 We <u>live</u> in flats.
2 They work in the evenings.
3 You like the same things.
4 I don't drive to the shops.

B Complete the table.

+	I You	like		sport.
–	We They	_____	live	in a house.

4 A Complete the sentences with a verb in the positive or negative.

1 I _____*live*_____ with a friend. (+)
2 I _____ two sisters. (+)
3 I _____ a camera. (–)
4 I _____ English five hours a week. (+)
5 I _____ in an office. (–)
6 I _____ James Bond films. (–)

B Tick the sentences above that are true for you. Change the sentences that aren't true.

1 I don't live with a friend. I live with my parents.

5 A Complete the tables with *do* or *don't*.

Where	_____	you		live?
What				study?

_____	you	have	a car?
Yes, I _____.		No, I _____.	

B ▶ 4.2 SENTENCE STRESS Listen and underline the stressed words.

A: <u>Where</u> do you <u>live</u>?
B: In London.
A: Do you live in a flat?
B: Yes, I do. And you?
A: No, I don't. I live in a house.

C Work in pairs and practise the conversation.

6 A Put the words in order to make questions.

1 cats / like / you / Do?
Do you like cats?
2 films / like / you / Do / American?
3 have / Do / a / you / dictionary?
4 you / like / Do / cola?
5 sports / like / do / you / What?
6 live / Where / you / do?

B Work in pairs and take turns. Ask and answer the questions.

▷ page 124 **LANGUAGEBANK**

SPEAKING

7 A Work alone and complete Column B about you.

A: Other students		B: You
1 _____*Lucie*_____	and	I like *Chinese food* .
2 _____	and	I have _____ .
3 _____	and	I live _____ .
4 _____	and	I don't like _____ .
5 _____	and	I don't have _____ .

B Work with other students. Ask questions to find students who are the same as you. Write their names in Column A.

A: *Do you like Chinese food?*
B: *Yes, I do.*
A: *Oh good. How do you spell your name?*
B: *L-u-c-i-e.*

C Tell the class the things you and other students have in common.

Lucie and I both like Chinese food.

WRITING

LINKERS AND, BECAUSE

8 A Read the blog entry. Which things are the same in your life?

My two cities

I'm from Toronto, Canada, but I work in Osaka, Japan, six months a year. I like life in Japan, but it's very different. In Toronto, I live in a big house and I drive to the shops because they're five kilometres from my house. In Osaka, I live in a small flat and I walk to work because I don't have a car. I'm often tired because we work six days a week.

B Complete the sentences with *and* or *because* Then check in the text.

1 I live in a big house _____ I drive to the shops.
2 I'm often tired _____ we work six days a week.

C Choose the correct ending.

Because answers the question *why/where*.

D Complete the sentences with *and* and *because*.

1 I like coffee _____ I have ten cups every day _____ it's cheap at my office.
2 I'm a waiter _____ I work in the city centre _____ all the restaurants are in the centre.
3 My English is good _____ I study a lot _____ I have a good teacher.

9 Write a blog entry about your life using five verbs from Exercise 1. Use *and* and *because*. Write 50–70 words.

4.2)) A GOOD MATCH

F present simple: *he/she/it*
P 3rd person s
V days; time phrases

Every week, we match two of our members and they meet for a date at a restaurant. This week's couple are Ben and Emma. We talk to them about their date.

What do you like about Emma?
She's beautiful and interesting. She's Spanish but she lives and works in Manchester.

Do you like the same things?
We both like football. I'm a Manchester City fan but Emma likes Barcelona. That's a problem, but not a big one.

Is family important to Emma?
I don't think family is important to Emma. She comes from a small family. She has one brother but she doesn't have any sisters. She works for a bank and I think her work is important to her.

What does she do in the evening and at the weekend?
In the week she goes to the gym or she cooks Spanish food for her friends. At the weekend she does different things, for example she plays tennis, and I think she's very good. She loves music and films – me too!

Where does she go on holiday?
She goes home to Spain or she goes to Italy. We both want to go to South America and Emma speaks Spanish of course. She likes beach holidays but I don't.

What do you like about Ben?
He's good-looking and friendly.

Do you like the same things?
Ben likes computer games but I don't. He plays guitar in a group and we like the same type of music. We both like football.

Is family important to Ben?
It's very important. Ben comes from a big family. He has two brothers and a sister and he loves children.

What does he do in the evening and at the weekend?
He doesn't go out in the week. He checks his students' homework and he watches TV. He goes out at the weekends. We both love films and music. And he plays tennis but he says he's not very good. He plays guitar with his group.

Where does he go on holiday?
He's a university teacher and he has long holidays. We both want to go to South America but he says it costs a lot of money. Ben doesn't like beach holidays but I love the beach.

READING

1 A Read the introduction and look at the photos of two people. Underline the correct alternatives.

1 The website is for finding a new *job/partner*.
2 Ben and Emma *work/meet* in a restaurant.

B Work in pairs. Student A: read Ben's answers. Student B: read Emma's answers. What three things do Ben and Emma have in common?

They both like …

C Work with other students and compare your answers.

2 A Work in pairs. Add words to make questions to ask Emma and Ben.

1 What / your job?
What's your job?
2 like football?
3 family / important / you?
4 What / do / in the evening?
5 What / do / at the weekend?
6 Where / go / on holiday?

B Student A: read Ben's interview again and answer questions 1–6 about Emma. Student B: read Emma's interview again and answer questions 1–6 about Ben.

C Work in pairs. Student A: you are Emma. Student B: you are Ben. Ask and answer questions 1–6. Find three differences between Ben and Emma.

A: Ben, what's your job?
B: I'm a teacher. What's your job?

GRAMMAR
PRESENT SIMPLE: *HE/SHE/IT*

3 A Underline the verbs in the sentences.

1 Emma lives and works in Manchester.
2 Ben watches TV.
3 He doesn't like beach holidays.

B Complete the table. Use the sentences above and the text in Exercise 1 to help.

+	He She It	come*s*_____ like_____ cost_____	from a big family. football. a lot of money.
	He	ha_____	two brothers.
–	He	_____ go	out in the week.
	She	_____ have	any sisters.

C Complete the rules.

> **RULES**
> 1 *He/she/it* + verb +_____
> 2 With *have*: use *he/she/it* + _____.
> 3 With verbs ending -*ch* and -*o*:
>   use verb + _____.
> 4 In the negative: use _____ + verb.

4 A ▶ 4.3 **3RD PERSON *s*** Listen and write the verbs.

B Which verbs end with /s/ /z/ /ɪz/ ? Listen and check. Then listen again and repeat.

▷ page 124 **LANGUAGEBANK**

5 A Complete the text with the correct form of the verb in brackets.

My name's Alex and my girlfriend Keira is very different from me. I ¹_____ (have) a small flat in the city centre, but she ²_____ (live) with her parents in the countryside. I ³_____ (work) as a doctor but she ⁴_____ (not have) a job and she ⁵_____ (have) a lot of free time. She ⁶_____ (not go) out in the evenings because it ⁷_____ (cost) a lot. We ⁸_____ (meet) at the weekends, but she ⁹_____ (not know) many of my friends. She ¹⁰_____ (say) she ¹¹_____ (love) me but she ¹²_____ (not want) to live in the city.

B Work in pairs and close your books. Write what you remember about Alex and Keira. Are they are a good match? Why?/Why not?

SPEAKING

6 A Work in pairs. Student A: turn to page 149. Student B: turn to page 153.

B Find five differences between Daniel and Yoshi, and one thing that is the same.

A: Daniel studies Chinese. How about Yoshi?
B: Yoshi studies English.

VOCABULARY
DAYS; TIME PHRASES

7 A Number the days of the week in order.

Monday ___*1*___
Saturday ___
Thursday ___
Wednesday ___
Sunday ___
Tuesday ___
Friday ___

B ▶ 4.4 Listen and check. Then listen again and repeat.

8 A Complete the table with *in, on, at* or *every*.

1	*every*	hour, day, week, month, Monday, weekend, morning
2	_____	the weekend, night
3	_____	the morning, the afternoon, the evening, a minute
4	_____	Monday, Wednesday

B Underline the correct alternatives.

1 I have coffee *in/on/every* morning.
2 I don't have coffee *in/on/every* the evening.
3 I meet my friends *in/at/on* Fridays and Saturdays.
4 I don't work *on/at/every* the weekend.
5 I study English *on/at/every* day.
6 I watch films *in/at/on* Sunday afternoons.

C Change the sentences above so that they are true for you. Then work in pairs and compare your answers. Find two things the same and two things that are different.

A: I have tea every morning.
B: I don't. I have coffee.

D Work with other students and tell them two things that are different.

A: I have tea every morning but Bernard has coffee.

4.3))) WHAT TIME IS IT?

F telling the time
P intonation for checking
V events

VOCABULARY

EVENTS

1 A Match the words in the box with events A–F.

> a film   a party   a play   a concert
> a festival   a match

B Work in pairs and take turns. Ask and answer about the events in the box.

A: *Do you like concerts?*
B: *No, I don't. What about you?*
A: *I don't like concerts, but I like plays.*

FUNCTION

TELLING THE TIME

2 A ▶ 4.5   Mia and Pete are in London for the weekend. Listen to their conversations and write the events in the order they talk about them.

1   *a concert*
2   _____
3   _____
4   _____
5   _____

B Listen again and complete Mia's diary.

	Saturday	Sunday
afternoon		
evening		

C Listen again and complete the conversations.

1 **B:** What's time is the concert?
  A: Let me check. It's at half past _____.
2 **B:** Do you want to go at six?
  A: Let's go at quarter to _____.
3 **B:** What time's the party?
  A: From _____ o'clock to six _____.
4 **A:** What time in the evening?
  B: Half _____ seven. Seven thirty.
5 **A:** I'm tired. What time is it?
  B: It's quarter past _____. Let's get a taxi.

▷ page 124 **LANGUAGEBANK**

3 A ▶ 4.6   Listen and repeat the times.

B Work in pairs and take turns. Student A: ask the time. Student B: say the time.

A: *What time is it in number one?*
B: *It's half past seven. What time … ?*

▷ page 142 **PHOTOBANK**

LEARN TO

CHECK TIMES

4 A Look at the conversation. How does the speaker check the time? Underline three sentences.

B: What time is the match?
A: It's at a quarter past two.
B: Sorry? What time?
A: Quarter past two.
B: Quarter past two. OK.

B ▶ 4.7 INTONATION: checking Look at the intonation in the questions. Then listen and repeat.

Sorry?   What time?

C Work in pairs and take turns. Student A: say one of the times below. Student B: check the time and write it.

| 9:30 | 5:30 | 8:15 | 7:45 | 11:30 | 7:30 |

A: *Quarter to eight.*
B: *Sorry? What time?*
A: *Quarter to eight.*
B: *Quarter to eight. Thanks.*

 **speakout TIP**

Use *sorry* in different ways in English: *Sorry?* = please repeat something. *I'm sorry I'm late.* = I feel bad because I'm late. You step on someone's foot = *Oh, I'm sorry*.

SPEAKING

5 A Work in pairs. Student A: look at the information below. Ask Student B to come to the events. Student B: turn to page 149.

Saturday	Sunday
10.15a.m. – film	
	1.45p.m. – play
9.30p.m. – party	

A: *Do you want to see a film on Saturday?*
B: *What film?*
A: *The new James Bond film.*
B: *What time does it start?*
A: *It starts at quarter past ten.*
B: *In the morning? OK! Let's go.*

B Student A: write the events and times that Student B suggests.

DVD PREVIEW

1 A Match the phrases 1–6 with the pictures A–F.

1 cut wood
2 collect eggs
3 travel by horse and carriage
4 go to a supermarket
5 eat at a fast food restaurant
6 use a modern machine

B Discuss in pairs. Which things in Exercise 1A do you do every week? Which things do you never do?

2 Read the programme information. Which things from Exercise 1A do you think the Amish family does? Which things do they never do?

◁)) Amish: a secret life   **BBC**

The Amish people live in Lancaster, Pennsylvania, USA. They have a traditional lifestyle, very different from other people in America. They don't use electricity or machines – no TV, no computers, no telephone and no cars. So how do they travel? What do they do in their free time? In this programme we visit an Amish family and learn about their day-to-day life.

DVD VIEW

3 A Watch the DVD and check your answers to Exercise 2.

B Work in pairs. Which three things below are not in the programme? Watch again and check.

| a car   a clock   an ATM   keys |
| a TV   a pen   a phone |

C Work in pairs and underline the correct alternative. Then watch the DVD again and check your answers.

1 This is my youngest *brother/son* Bennon.
2 We've got *visitors/friends*.
3 This is Katie. This is our oldest *daughter/sister*.
4 It's dark in the house because the Amish don't use *electricity/machines*.
5 It takes at least five minutes to get my *horse/carriage* out, and the children.
6 But they also go into town and shop at *normal/special* shops.
7 The traditional Amish in Lancaster County don't have phones in their *kitchens/houses* …
8 … he's happiest when he's at home and his *children are/family is* all together …

D Work in pairs and discuss. What's one thing you like about the Amish lifestyle?

speakout a group survey

4 A Work in pairs and read the information a)–h) about the Amish lifestyle. Then discuss questions 1 and 2.

1 Do you think it's a good thing or a bad thing? Write G or B.

2 Is your life similar or different?

a) they don't have a computer or a TV

b) they work outside

c) they live in the countryside

d) they don't drive

e) the woman does the housework

f) the man has a job

g) the children help around the house

h) the family is together a lot

B ▶ 4.8 Listen to three people doing a group survey. Tick (✓) the topics a)–h) they talk about. How many people say these things are good?

C Listen again and tick the key phrases you hear.

> **KEY PHRASES**
>
> I'll go first/next.
>
> My question is about [e) and f)/the computer/the man and the woman].
>
> Do you think that's a good thing?
>
> Why? Why not?
>
> In my family, this is normal.
>
> I think it's [OK/a good thing/a good idea/a bad thing/a problem].
>
> I think you're right./I agree with you.
>
> I don't agree with you.

5 A Work in groups. Each student: choose two topics from Exercise 4A. Ask the other students their opinion. Make notes of their answers.

B Tell the class the results of your survey.

In our group, two people think working outside is a bad thing.
One person thinks it's a good thing.
OR
We all think it's a good/bad thing.

writeback a report

6 A Complete the report with topics from Exercise 4A.

> ## THE AMISH LIFESTYLE
>
> 1 _____
>
> In our group two people think it is a good thing because it's important for a family to do things together, for example to eat together. One person thinks it's a problem because children need time alone.
>
> 2 _____
>
> We all think this is a good idea because children learn that work is important and the woman doesn't do all the housework.

B Write a report (50–70 words) on the two topics you talked about in Exercise 5A. Use the reports above to help Write 80–100 words.

Ⓥ VERB PHRASES

1 A Cross out the word or phrase that is <u>not</u> correct.

1 I like *cats/people/~~late~~*.
2 You work *in pairs/city/in an office*.
3 We go *university/to English lessons/to the gym*.
4 They have *a car/a problem/hungry*.
5 You live *a flat/in Hong Kong/alone*.
6 We study *Spanish/five hours a week/bored*.
7 I drive *a sports car/work/a taxi*.
8 They do *tennis/sport/homework*.

B Think of a good friend. What do you have in common? Write three sentences using the verbs above.

Sonia is a good friend from university. We are twenty-three and we work in the city. We both like the cinema.

C Work in pairs and take turns. Read your sentences.

Ⓖ PRESENT SIMPLE: I/YOU/WE/THEY

2 A Use the table to write four questions.

Do	you	like ...?
	your friends	work ...?
		read ...?
	you and your friends	do ...?
		live ...?
	the other students in the class	watch ...?
		have ...?
		go ...?

1 Do you and your friends watch films together?

B Work in pairs and take turns. Ask and answer your questions.

Ⓖ PRESENT SIMPLE: HE/SHE/IT

3 A Complete the sentences.

1 He / not / work / hotel
He doesn't work in a hotel.
2 She / live / in a flat
3 He / not / like / hamburgers
4 She / have / a brother
5 He / not / like / shopping
6 She / do / sport / at the weekend

B Work in pairs. Change *he/she* in sentences 1–6 above. Write the names of students in your class.

1 Abel doesn't work in a hotel.
2 Patrizia lives in a flat.

C Check the information with the students. How many sentences are correct about the students?

A: Abel, do you work in a hotel?
B: No, I don't.

Ⓥ DAYS; TIME PHRASES

4 A Write the days of the week.

Mo Tu We Th Fr Sa Su
Monday

B Match the times 1–6 with the phrases a)–f).

1 Monday, Monday, Monday *c*
2 9a.m.
3 Saturday and Sunday
4 3p.m.
5 9p.m.
6 Monday–Sunday

a) at the weekend
b) in the evening
c) every Monday
d) in the morning
e) every day
f) in the afternoon

C Write something you do at the times in Exercise 4B.

I do sport every Monday.

D Work in pairs and take turns. Student A: say an activity. Student B: guess the time.

A: I do sport.
B: In the evening?
A: No.
B: Every Monday?
A: Yes!

Ⓥ EVENTS

5 A Add vowels to complete the events.

1 f *i* lm
2 c__nc__rt
3 p__rty
4 pl__y
5 f__st__v__l
6 m__tch

B Work in pairs and take turns. Student A: choose an event and say words to help. Student B: guess the event.

A: Music, dancing …
B: A party?
A: No.
B: A festival?
A: Yes!

Ⓕ TELLING THE TIME

6 A Write the times in words.

1 5.45 ___quarter to six___
2 12.30 _____
3 7.15 _____
4 3.00 _____
5 3.45 _____
6 11.15 _____

B Write six times in numbers.

C Work in pairs and take turns. Student A: read your times. Student B: write them in numbers. Then check.

A: Half past three.
B: (writes) 2.30
A: (checks) No, it's 3.30.

LISTENING AND GRAMMAR

1 A Match the words in the box with the icons.

> cafés *F* clothes films people
> places websites

 A
 B
 C
 D
 E
 F

B Work in pairs and take turns. Student A: choose one icon and give an example. Student B: say the icon.

A: *Star Wars.*
B: *Films.*
A: *Correct.*
B: *My daughter Anna.*
A: *People.*

2 A ▷ C2.1 Listen to a woman talking about her favourite things and people. Number the icons in Exercise 1A in order.

B Listen again. How many things or people does she talk about for each icon?

cafés _____
clothes _____
films _____
people ___*3*___
places _____
websites _____

3 A Add words to make sentences. Use the correct form of the verbs.

1 Alicia / be / Beth / sister   *Alicia is Beth's sister.*
2 William / say / Alicia / be / beautiful
3 Beth / know / Keith / from university
4 Beth / Monique / be / not / friends
5 Beth / have / red party dress
6 She / like / the BBC website
7 She / go / the Gelatino Café / every day

B Work in pairs. Which sentence in Exercise 3A is false? Check the audio script on page 156.

SPEAKING

4 A Choose three words in the box to write in the table 1–3.

> people   places   restaurants   cafés   clothes   music
> films   animals

My favourites		
1 _____	2 _____	3 _____

B Complete your table with three things or people for each group.

C Work with other students and take turns. Ask and answer about your favourite things and people.

A: *What are your groups?*
B: *Places, clothes, music.*
A: *OK. What are your favourite places?*
B: *Rome, Milan and London.*
A: *Oh, why?*
B: *I like cities. Rome is very old and beautiful …*

READING AND GRAMMAR

5 A Read the description of Keith and Alicia. What are their jobs? What is their favourite thing about their jobs? What don't they like?

My friend Keith works alone. He works from three in the afternoon to twelve at night every day, but he doesn't have time to stop or to eat. He meets people from many different countries. He goes to and from the airport five or six times every day and has about twenty different customers in his car. He also drives people around the city and he knows it very well. Keith likes his job. He says that his favourite part is the people, but he doesn't like working in the evenings and he gets very tired at the end of his day.

My sister Alicia's job isn't very difficult. On a typical day, she sits at her desk from nine to five and welcomes people when they come in. She checks their names, nationalities and car number plates and then gives them their room key. What else? She answers the phone, reads and writes emails and takes people's money when they go. She says she likes her job because every day is different but she doesn't like her work clothes: a white shirt and red trousers.

B Who says 1–8 below? Keith (K) or Alicia (A)?

1 No, I don't have special clothes for work. *K*
2 No, I don't work in office.
3 Yes, I do. I speak on the phone a lot.
4 Yes, I use a computer in my job.
5 No, I don't work in the evenings.
6 Yes, I drive a lot in my job.

C Look at Exercise 5B again. Write the questions.

1 Do you have special clothes for work?

D Write two things you have in common with Keith and Alicia. Write two things that are different.

E Work in pairs. Compare your day with Keith's and Alicia's.

Keith drives in his job, but I don't. Alicia works at a desk and I do, too.

SPEAKING

6 A Work in groups. Write the names of ten jobs.

B Work in groups and take turns. Student A: choose a job. Other students: ask questions to find the job.

B: Do you have special clothes for work? **A:** *Yes, I do.*
C: Do you work in a hospital? **A:** *No, I don't.*

SOUNDS: /s/ AND /z/

7 A ▶ C2.2 Listen to the sounds and the words. Then listen again and repeat.

/s/	/z/
cake**s**	coffee**s**

B ▶ C2.3 Listen and put the words in the box in the correct group. Then listen again and repeat.

| tea~~s~~ spark**i**ng ha**s** **s**andwich euro**s** **s**port |
| drive**s** thi**s** |

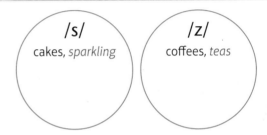

/s/
cakes, *sparkling*

/z/
coffees, *teas*

8 A Work in pairs. Circle the word with a different *s* sound.

1 (this) these, those
2 Jack's, Pat's, Tom's
3 sweater, trousers, hats
4 it's, he's, she's
5 books, bags, cups
6 goes, does, likes

B ▶ C2.4 Listen and check. Then listen again and repeat.

C Complete the rules with /s/ or /z/ for the pronunciation of *s*.

| RULES | 1 At the beginning of words: _____
2 At the end of words, after /k/, /t/ and /p/: _____
3 At the end of words, after /d/, /m/, /g/, /v/, /l/, /n/: _____ |

9 A Underline sixteen examples of the letter *s* in the sentences.

/s/
1 My **s**on lives near the sea and the mountains.
2 The lamps and the clocks are in the rooms near the beds.
3 Can I have six eggs, please?
4 Sue emails her parents on Sundays.

B How is the *s* pronounced in each word? Write /s/ or /z/. Use the rules in Exercise 8C to help.

C ▶ C2.5 Listen and check. Then listen again and repeat.

5 routines

BAD HABITS p52

YOU ARE WHAT YOU EAT p54

WHEN DOES IT OPEN? p56

HOW TO FEED YOUR KIDS p58

BBC

BBC INTERVIEWS

◁)) What do you usually do at the weekend?

G present simple questions: *he/she/it*
P weak form: *does*
V daily routines

VOCABULARY
DAILY ROUTINES

1 A ▶ 5.1 Listen and match the sounds with the verbs in the box.

> get up *1* go to bed have dinner
> go to work have lunch get home
> have breakfast

B Work in pairs and take turns. Ask and answer about your daily routines.

A: *What time do you have breakfast in the morning?*
B: *At seven o'clock in the week and at nine o'clock on Saturday and Sunday. And you?*
A: *I have breakfast at …*

▷ page 143 **PHOTOBANK**

speakout TIP

Practice helps you to remember. Write seven sentences about your daily routine in your phrasebook. Practise saying them every day.

LISTENING

2 A Work in pairs and look at the photos. Who is angry and why?

B ▶ 5.2 Listen and match conversations 1–3 with photos A–C.

1 _____ 2 _____ 3 _____

C Listen again and tick one true sentence. Correct the false sentences.

1 Clara has a job.
Clara doesn't have a job.
2 Clara gets up at twelve at the weekend.
3 Clara talks to her parents.
4 Julio listens to Paula.
5 Paula doesn't talk about her problems.
6 Wayne's neighbour works at night.
7 Wayne's neighbour gets home at five.
8 Wayne gets up at eight o'clock.

D Work in pairs. Do you have these problems with family, friends, neighbours or people at work? Tell your partner about the problems.

GRAMMAR
PRESENT SIMPLE QUESTIONS: *HE/SHE/IT*

3 A Complete the tables with *does* and *doesn't*.

What time When		she he	get up? go to bed?
What		it	mean?

		she he	have a job? play loud music?
Yes, he/she _____.		No, he/she _____.	

B ▶ 5.3 **WEAK FORM:** *does* Look at the pronunciation of *does he/she/it* in the questions. Is *does* stressed or unstressed? Then listen again and repeat.

1 What does it mean? /dəzɪt/
2 When does he go to bed? /dəzi/
3 Does she have a job? /dəʃɪ/

▷ page 126 **LANGUAGEBANK**

4 Add *does* in four places in each conversation.

1 **A:** What time ~~does~~ Mike come home in the evenings?

   B: At about eight o'clock.

   A: So, he play with the children?

   B: No, he doesn't. They go to bed at seven.

   A: And he work at the weekends?

   B: Yes, he, or he goes out and plays golf!

2 **A:** Ana, your sister phone you on your birthday?

   B: No, she doesn't.

   A: When she phone you?

   B: On her birthday because she wants money!

   A: Really? So it drive you crazy?

   B: Yes, it.

5 A Complete the questions with the verbs in the box.

~~like~~   study   go (x2)   watch   have (x2)   listen
do   read

1 (he) _____Does he like_____ parties?
2 (she) _____ her homework every day?
3 (he) _____ a job?
4 (she) _____ at university?
5 (your teacher) _____ a newspaper every day?
6 (you) _____ to the radio?
7 (your sister) _____ DVDs a lot?
8 (he) _____ to concerts a lot?
9 (she) _____ lunch in this building?
10 (you) _____ to bed after midnight?

B Choose five questions from Exercise 5A. Add the names of students in your class.

1 Does Marcus like parties?

C Work in pairs and take turns to ask and answer. If you don't know, ask the person or say *I don't know.*

A: *Does Marcus like parties?*
B: *I don't know. Excuse me, Marcus. Do you like parties?*
C: *Yes, I do.*
B: *Yes, he does. Does Rachel …*

SPEAKING

6 A Work in pairs. Ask and answer the questions in the quiz below. Put a tick when your partner answers yes. Who has more bad habits?

10 bad habits that drive people crazy

Do you …

talk a lot and not listen?
look at your phone all the time?
stay in the bathroom for hours?
talk in films?
eat on trains?
sing in the bathroom?
take selfies (photos of yourself) all the time?
play very loud music in the car or at home?
smoke?
drive very fast?

B Put the bad habits in order 1–10 from <u>really</u> bad (1) to not so bad (10). Then discuss with your partner. Do not look at your partner's book.

C Work with other students. Do you know any people with these bad habits? What other bad habits do they have?

A: *My brother sings in the bathroom. He's a very bad singer!*
B: *Does he have any other bad habits?*
A: *Yes, he takes photos of himself all the time!*

5.2)) YOU ARE WHAT YOU EAT

G adverbs of frequency
P word stress
V food

VOCABULARY

FOOD

1 A Match the words with photos A–J.

1	pasta	J	**6**	fruit	____
2	steak	____	**7**	vegetables	____
3	chicken	____	**8**	eggs	____
4	rice	____	**9**	cheese	____
5	fish	____	**10**	biscuits	____

B WORD STRESS Underline the stressed syllable in the food items above. Then write the number of syllables (1, 2 or 3) next to each word.

pasta 2

C ▶ 5.4 Listen and check. Then listen and repeat.

2 Work in pairs and take turns to ask questions. What food do you both like?

A: I like steak. Do you?
B: No, I don't. Do you like pasta?
A: Yes, I do.

▷ page 143 **PHOTOBANK**

READING

3 A Work in pairs. Look at the photos of the two people. Which of these foods do you think they <u>both</u> eat every day?

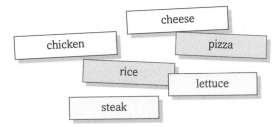

B Read the texts and check your ideas.

Byron Hanson
SWIMMER

I'm never hungry because I eat a lot. I need about 6,000 calories a day, and I eat six meals every day. My breakfast is at 6a.m. and I usually have three eggs, some milk, cereal and fish oil. For lunch I have the same thing every day. I always have fish or steak (sometimes I have both!) and I have peppers, cheese and pasta. For dinner I have chicken with a lot of rice, some cheese and lots of vegetables – tomatoes, lettuce and peppers. I love junk food but I never eat it.

Petra Leon
SUPERMODEL

I love food and I don't have a strict diet. I love steak but I don't often eat it, maybe twice a month. I eat a lot of raw food, and I never eat tinned food. I usually have a small breakfast of toast, and for lunch I have chicken and rice, lettuce and fruit. For dinner I have fish, salad and fruit. I often snack between meals, usually biscuits, fruit and cheese, and I drink fruit juice. I have dinner three hours before I go to bed because that helps me sleep.

C Read the texts again and answer the questions. Write B (Byron), P (Petra) or BP (Byron and Petra). Who …

1 loves food? *BP*
2 snacks a lot?
3 doesn't eat tinned food?
4 has a big breakfast?
5 talks about steak and chicken?
6 likes junk food?
7 eats a lot of fruit?

D Discuss in pairs. Is your diet similar to Byron's or Petra's? How is your diet different from theirs?

GRAMMAR

ADVERBS OF FREQUENCY

4 A Underline the words in the box in the text from Exercise 3B.

sometimes   always   never   often   not often   usually

B Put the words in the box in the correct place on the line below. Use the texts in Exercise 3 to help you.

```
100%
 80%
 60%
 40%        sometimes
 10%
  0%
```

C ▶ 5.5 **WORD STRESS** Listen and underline the stress in the adverbs. Then listen and repeat.

always

D Look at sentences 1–3. Underline the correct alternatives in the rules.

1 I'm **never** hungry because I eat a lot.
2 I love steak but I do**n't often** eat it …
3 I **usually** have a small breakfast …

> **RULES**
> **1** The adverb goes *before/after* the verb 'be'.
> **2** The adverb goes *before/after* 'don't' and 'doesn't'.
> **3** The adverb goes *before/after* other verbs.

▷ page 126 **LANGUAGEBANK**

5 A Put the words in the correct order to make sentences.

1 have / usually / I / Fridays / on / fish
I usually have fish on Fridays.
2 eat / never / I / sweets
3 hungry / I'm / never
4 eat / often / chicken / I
5 home / dinner / for / usually / I'm
6 fruit / eat / don't / I / often
7 have / sometimes / I / lunch / for / vegetables
8 I / eat / Sundays / steak / always / on

B Work in pairs. Which sentences are true for you? Change the other sentences to make them true.

SPEAKING

6 A Read the sentences below. Complete them with *always* (A), *usually* (U), *sometimes* (S), *not often* (NO) and *never* (N).

In the morning, I …
· have a coffee before breakfast.
· have a big breakfast.
· make a sandwich for lunch.
· read my emails.
· drive to work/school.

In the evening, I …
· cook dinner for my family.
· eat after eight o'clock.
· watch TV for two hours.
· go out with friends.
· have a hot drink before I go to bed.

B Work in pairs and compare your answers. Find two things in common.

A: I never have a coffee before breakfast. What about you?
B: I never drink coffee.

C What other things do you usually do in the morning and evening?

WRITING

LINKERS TO SEQUENCE

7 A Read the description. Is it similar to your morning?

> ## My morning
>
> Every day I get up at six. First, I make a black coffee and I read my emails. Then I have breakfast and listen to the radio. I usually have cereal and coffee but I sometimes have toast and an egg. After that, I often read the news online. Finally, at half past eight I go to work. I always walk to work because it's only fifteen minutes to my office. At work I have another coffee and sometimes a cake.

B Read the description again and number the linkers in order.

then   first *1*   finally   after that

C Which linker does <u>not</u> have a comma after it?

speakout TIP

Linkers are very important in writing. They connect ideas and help your writing become clearer. Which of these words is NOT a linker?
and, but, first, because, at, then

8 A Write a description of your typical morning. Use linkers and write 60–80 words.

B Read other students' descriptions. Are they similar to your morning?

5.3)) WHEN DOES IT OPEN?

F asking for information
P sentence stress
V hotel services

A

VOCABULARY

HOTEL SERVICES

1 A Look at the photos. Which services in the box are in photos A–D?

> a restaurant   a gym   a café   a gift shop
> a money exchange   a hairdresser's
> a swimming pool   a guided tour

B Match the services from the box with activities 1–8.

1 have dinner *a restaurant*   5 have a coffee
2 change money   6 go swimming
3 get a haircut   7 buy gifts
4 do exercise   8 see the town

C Discuss in pairs. Which two services are important in a hotel? Which two aren't important?

FUNCTION

ASKING FOR INFORMATION

2 A ▶ 5.6   Listen to the conversations. Which four services does the woman ask about?

1 *a gym*   3 _____
2 _____   4 _____

B Listen again. Find and correct the five mistakes in the woman's notes.

> gym: 6a.m.–9p.m.
> closes: 12–1
> breakfast?: 6.30–9.00; in café
> hairdresser's: 10–6; Tuesday to 8p.m.;
> closes Mondays.
> Guided tour: 9a.m. and 2p.m. €50.

3 A ▶ 5.7   Complete the conversation. Then listen and check.

A: When does the gym ¹ _*open*_ ?
B: It ² _____ from 6a.m. to 10p.m.
A: What ³ _____ is breakfast?
B: From half past six ⁴ _____ nine o'clock.
A: ⁵ _____ you have a hairdresser's in the hotel?
B: Yes, it opens ⁶ _____ day except Monday.
A: When ⁷ _____ the tour leave?
B: It ⁸ _____ at 9a.m. and at 3p.m.
A: How much does it ⁹ _____ ?
B: ¹⁰ _____ costs fifteen euros.

B SENTENCE STRESS Work in pairs and underline the stressed words. Listen again and check. Then listen and repeat.

1 When does the gym open?

▷ page 126 **LANGUAGEBANK**

4 A Add words to make a conversation.

Student A

> When / gift shop / open?

Student B

> 10a.m.–8p.m.

> Swimming pool / open / all day?

> Yes, it / open / 6a.m.–9p.m. but it / close / 12–1p.m.

> How much / guided tour / cost / for children?

> It / be / free / for children.

> When / it / leave?

> It / leave / 10a.m.

B Work in pairs and take turns. Practise the conversation.

B

C

D

LEARN TO

USE TWO-PART EXCHANGES

5 A Look at sentences 1–6 from the conversation in Exercise 2A. Who says them? Write receptionist (R) or guest (G).

1 I'm sorry, but your room isn't ready. *R*
   a) That's a shame.   **b)** Great, thanks.

2 Breakfast is in the restaurant, over there.
   a) Enjoy your meal!   **b)** Right. Thank you.

3 Thank you.
   a) You're welcome.   **b)** I do.

4 We do a tour from the hotel.
   a) Have fun!   **b)** Great, thanks.

5 Do you have a map of the city?
   a) Yes, here you are.   **b)** Good idea!

6 Have a nice day.
   a) Two please.   **b)** You too.

B Look at the answers above. Tick the correct answer a) or b).

C ▷ 5.8 Listen and check. Then listen and repeat the answers.

D Work in pairs. Student A: say a phrase from 1–6 in Exercise 5A. Student B: cover Exercise 5A and answer. Then swap.

speakout TIP

Write two-part exchanges in your phrasebook to help you in typical situations. What is a typical answer to:

1 *How are you?*
2 *Nice to meet you.*
3 *Let's have a break.*

SPEAKING

6 A Work in pairs. You are tourists at a hotel in Prague. Make questions about the times and/or the prices. You want to:

change money.	*What time does the money exchange open?*
have coffee at Café Slavia or Café Milena.	
have lunch at the hotel.	
go on a guided tour of Prague.	
go to the opera.	

B Work with a new partner. Student A: you are the tourist. Ask Student B your questions and write the answers. Student B: turn to page 150 and answer the questions.

C Change roles. Student A: turn to page 152 and answer the questions. Student B: ask your questions and write the answers.

D Check your partner's information. Is it correct?

DVD PREVIEW

1 A Match the words in the box with photos A–F.

> nuts   raisins   sweets   mango   biscuits   crisps

B Work in pairs. Which snacks in the photos are healthy? Which snacks do you usually never eat?

2 A Read the programme information and tick two correct answers for each item.

1   The programme is about
   a) children.   **b)** exercise.   **c)** snacks.
2   In this programme there is an experiment about
   a) saying 'no'.   **b)** children's eating habits.
   c) healthy snacks.

B Work in pairs and answer the last two questions in the programme information.

◁)) How to feed your kids

BBC

What do you think about children and food? Do kids like healthy food? Do they snack too much? The BBC programme *How to feed your kids* is about children and food, and how to change kids' eating habits. One experiment looks at the questions: Is it a good idea to say 'no' to a snack? Is saying 'no' good or bad for kids' snacking habits?

DVD VIEW

3 A Watch the DVD and choose the correct sentence endings.

1   Before the experiment …
   a) … the kids like raisins more.
   b) … the kids like mangoes more.
   c) … the kids like raisins and mangoes the same.
2   After the experiment …
   a) … the kids like raisins more.
   b) … the kids like mangoes more.
   c) … the kids like raisins and mangoes the same.

B Work in pairs and underline the correct alternative. Then watch the DVD again and check your answers.

1   In this experiment, you need: *one class/school*, twenty *children/kids*, and two snacks …
2   After that, at the *first/second* whistle, the children can eat the raisins.
3   It's Day One and the children want the *raisins/ mangoes*.
4   On Day Ten, the kids are raisin crazy. They're *fruit/ animals*!
5   Then we ask all the children *together/in a group*. Which is your favourite snack?
6   Say *'no'/'yes'* and children want the snacks more.

speakout desert island food

4 A Read the text from a food forum and write your list.

 You have ten years on a desert island. The island has fresh water but no food. What types of food and drink do you take with you? The maximum is five types of food and two drinks. Send us your list!

B ▶ 5.9 Listen to a woman talking about her list. What food and drink does she talk about?

C Listen again and tick the key phrases you hear.

> **KEY PHRASES**
>
> What's on your list?
> Number [one/two/three/…] on my list is …
> It's [good/bad] for you …
> Do you really like …?
> I really like …
> I don't like [it/fruit/eggs/…].
> Really?
> What about drinks?
> Me too.

5 A Work in pairs and take turns to talk about your lists. Use the key phrases to help.

B Work in groups and take turns. One student: talk about your list. Other students: listen and ask one question.

writeback a forum entry

6 A Read the reply to the forum question. Then work in pairs and answer the questions.

1 Are these things on your list?
2 Which things on the list <u>don't</u> you like?

My food is very simple because I don't cook, and I love sandwiches.

Here's my list:

bread – I always have sandwiches for lunch, and I need bread for sandwiches.

cheese – A cheese sandwich is easy to make.

chicken – I think meat is important, and I love chicken. Chicken is also good in a sandwich.

apples – I don't like apples but they're good for you. Apples are good with cheese too.

tomatoes – They're my favourite food, and great in sandwiches!

coffee – I usually start every day with a black coffee.

orange juice – Very important for vitamin C!

B Write your list and give one reason for each item.

ⓥ DAILY ROUTINES

1 A Complete the word webs with a verb from the box

go get have

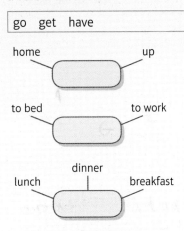

home | up

to bed | to work

lunch | dinner | breakfast

B Work in pairs and take turns. Cover the verbs. Student A: say three verb phrases from Exercise 1A. Student B: say the same verb phrases in the order you do them.

A: go to bed, have breakfast, get home

B: One I have breakfast, two I get home, and three I go to bed.

ⓖ PRESENT SIMPLE QUESTIONS: *HE/SHE/IT*

2 A Add words to make questions.

1 When / he / get up?
   When does he get up?

2 she / like / coffee / or / tea?
   _____

3 What time / he / go / to work?
   _____

4 What / she / have / for lunch?
   _____

5 he / have / a car?
   _____

6 When / she / get home?
   _____

7 she / study / at the weekend?
   _____

8 he / phone / you / every day?
   _____

B Work in pairs and take turns. Student A: ask questions. Student B: answer about a person in your family or a friend.

A: Who is your person?
B: My wife, Vanessa.
A: OK. When does she get up?

ⓥ FOOD

3 A Correct the spelling of the food words.

1	egs *eggs*	6	fis
2	chiken	7	stake
3	chees	8	rise
4	pastar	9	vegtables
5	biscits	10	friut

B Write three food words in each circle.

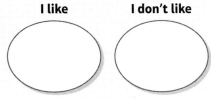

I like | I don't like

I don't eat

C Work in pairs and take turns. Student A: say one of your foods. Student B: guess if Student A likes it, doesn't like it or doesn't eat it.

A: Steak.
B: You don't like it.
A: No, I don't eat it.

ⓖ ADVERBS OF FREQUENCY

4 A Find and correct the mistakes. One sentence is correct.

1 We speak English together always in class.

2 I usually do my homework.

3 I'm late never for English lessons.

4 I not often watch English videos.

5 My English teacher says often 'Good!'

6 I read an online English newspaper never.

7 I'm not tired usually in English lessons.

B Tick the sentences that are true for you. Change the others to make them true. Then compare with a partner.

1 We don't always speak English together in class. We sometimes speak Italian.

ⓥ HOTEL SERVICES

5 Find and circle eight hotel services.

ⓕ ASKING FOR INFORMATION

6 A Look at the times of the hotel services. Complete questions 1–4.

1 What time _____ the gym close?

2 When _____ the café open?

3 _____ does the gift shop open _____ Mondays?

4 _____ does the swimming pool open and close?

B Work alone. Complete the timetable a)–d) with times.

Hotel services

a) gym
8a.m.–_____ Mon-Sat (S̶u̶n̶)

b) café
_____–10p.m. Mon-Sun

c) gift shop
11a.m.–7p.m. Tue-Sun (M̶o̶n̶)

d) swimming pool
_____–_____ (Mon-Sun)

C Work in pairs and take turns. Ask and answer questions 1–4.

6)) journeys

NO TRAINS p62

GETTING THERE p64

SINGLE OR RETURN? p66

RUSH HOUR p68

B B C
INTERVIEWS

)) How do you get to school or work?

6.1))) NO TRAINS

G *there is/are*
P word stress; sentence stress
V places

VOCABULARY

PLACES

1 A Match the words in the box with pictures A–H.

> an internet café C   a newsagent's H
> a hotel A a café   a restaurant
> a pharmacy   a payphone
> a cash machine G

B ▶ **6.1 WORD STRESS** Listen to the places and underline the stressed syllable(s). Then listen and repeat.

an <u>in</u>ternet <u>ca</u>fé

C Work in pairs and take turns. Ask and answer about the pictures in Exercise 1A.

A: *What's G?*
B: *It's a cash machine. What's … ?*

▷ page 144 **PHOTOBANK**

LISTENING

2 A Do you like train travel? What's good and what's bad about it?

A: *I like it because …*

B ▶ **6.2** Listen to the conversations and number the places in Exercise 1A in the order you hear them. Two places are <u>not</u> in the conversations.

payphone 1

C Listen again and underline the correct alternative.

1 The weather is *cold/<u>bad</u>*.
2 The man's phone is *dead/broken*.
3 The internet café *is/<u>isn't</u>* in the station.
4 The restaurants are *closed/expensive*.
5 The Charlotte Street Hotel is *full/<u>expensive</u>*.

GRAMMAR

THERE IS/ARE

3 A Complete the table with the words in the box.

> 's Are are isn't Is there aren't

	singular	plural
+	There ___'s___ a payphone over there	There _are_ two hotels near here.
-	There isn't an internet café.	There _aren't_ any trains.
?	_Is_ there a train to York tonight?	_Are_ there any restaurants in the station?
?	Yes, there is. No, there _isn't_	Yes, there are. No, _there_ aren't.

B ▶ **6.3** Listen and check.

C SENTENCE STRESS Listen again and underline two or three main stresses in each sentence. Then listen and repeat.

▷ page 128 **LANGUAGEBANK**

4 A Complete the sentences about a class with *There's*, *There are*, *There isn't* or *There aren't*.

1 ___*There are*___ three students with black shoes. (+)
2 ___There's___ one person with a red T-shirt. (+)
3 ___There isn't___ a whiteboard. (–)
4 ___There are___ two women in this room. (+)
5 ___There's___ a book on the teacher's desk. (+)
6 ___There aren't___ any dictionaries. (–)

B Work in pairs. Which sentences are true about your class?

5

A Work in pairs. Student A: write questions about places near the class. Student B: write questions about places near Student A's home.

1 pharmacy?
2 internet café?
3 a newsagent's?
4 any restaurants?
5 cash machine?
6 any clothes shops?

B Work in pairs and take turns. Ask and answer the questions.

A: Is there a pharmacy near here?
B: Yes, there is. It's two minutes from here. Its name is …

SPEAKING

6

Work in pairs. Student A: look at the picture on page 151. Student B: look at the picture on page 152.

7

A Think of a street in a town you know well. Draw a simple map or picture of the street. Write the name of five places on the picture.

B Work with other students. Look at their pictures and ask questions.

A: What's the name of this restaurant?
B: It's Primo Pizzeria.
A: Is it good?
B: Yes, it's my favourite place for pizza. Is there a restaurant on your street?
A: Yes, here it is. It's …

WRITING

STARTING AND ENDING AN EMAIL

8

A Read the email. Is the email to the man's manager, friend or someone in his family?

> Hi Sue,
>
> I have good news and bad news. There aren't any trains tonight because the weather's very bad. That's the bad news. So what's the good news? I'm in a very good hotel and there's a nice restaurant, too. Yes, it's expensive, but I have the company credit card.
>
> Give my love to mum. See you at her birthday party tomorrow.
>
> Take care,
>
> Pete

B Complete the table with phrases for starting and ending an email.

~~Hi Valentina,~~ ~~Best wishes, (x2)~~ Hello,
Take care, Dear Jack, See you soon,
Dear Mr Wilson, Regards,

	to someone close (a family member, partner, friends)	to your manager
Start	*Hi Valentina,* Hello	*Dear Mr Wilson, dear Jack*
End	*Best wishes,* see you soon Take care	*Best wishes,* Regards

9

A Work in pairs. Which problems often happen to you when you travel?

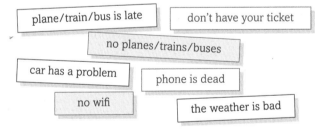

plane/train/bus is late
don't have your ticket
no planes/trains/buses
car has a problem
phone is dead
no wifi
the weather is bad

A: When I travel my bus is often late.
B: Yes, buses in the city are very bad.

B Choose two of the problems above. Write an email to a friend or to your manager. Write about your problems.

C Read other students' emails. Which situation is *really* bad?

VOCABULARY

TRANSPORT

1 A Write the transport words in the box under pictures A–H.

> a bus   a train   a plane   a taxi   the underground
> a car   a bike   a motorbike

 A
a bus

 B
a taxi

 C
a car

 D
a bike

 E
a train

 F
a plane

 G
the underground

 H
a motorbike

B Work in pairs and answer the questions.

1 How do you usually come to class?

I come by bus or I sometimes walk.

2 What types of transport do you use every week?

3 What types of transport do you use on holiday?

4 What types of transport do you never use?

READING

2 A Read the text and complete the headings with words from Exercise 1A.

B Write the name of the place and/or transport.

1 It doesn't have any stations.   *Bhutan*

2 It's not a good idea to drink a lot here. *on a plane*

3 These are expensive in bad weather. *taxis in Rome*

4 It's a noisy place to play. *a golf course in an airport in Thailand*

5 It's a good thing there are no cats. *the London Underground*

6 Men don't use these. *pink taxis in Moscow/Chennai*

7 It's not easy to get to those villages. *the villages in Bhutan*

8 That means turning nine times every kilometre! *the Tianmen Mountain Road in China*

C Work in pairs and discuss. Which facts are surprising? Which 'fact' is not true?

It's surprising that there are taxis for women. I think it's a good idea.

Transport facts around the world

Travel by *taxi*

- There are pink taxis in Moscow, Chennai (India), and a lot of other cities. The pink taxis are for women only, and the drivers are women.

- In Madagascar, taxi drivers often stop for petrol and the passenger pays.

- In Rome, a taxi fare is double when it rains.

Travel by *bus, train* and *train*

- There aren't any trains in the country of Bhutan in Asia. There are buses, but some villages don't have buses.

- There are a lot of mice in the London Underground – about 500,000!

- More than half of the London Underground is not underground.

Travel by *car*

- Venice, Italy has a secret road system, and people usually travel around Venice by car.

- An eleven kilometre section of the Tianmen Mountain Road in Hunan, China has ninety-nine bends.

Travel by *a plane*

- In Thailand, there's an airport with a golf course in it.

- One airline plans to charge passengers for using the toilet.

GRAMMAR

A/AN, SOME, A LOT OF, NOT ANY

3 A Look at the sentences. Match the words in bold with pictures A–D.

1 In Thailand, there's **an** airport with a golf course in it.   *B*
2 There are**n't any** trains in the country of Bhutan.
3 **Some** villages don't have a bus service.
4 There are **a lot of** mice in the London Underground.

B Complete the table with 's, are, isn't or aren't.

+	There	is	a	train at four o'clock.
		are	some	buses this afternoon.
		are	a lot of	cars.
–	There	is	an	airport here.
		are	any	cars in the centre.
?	is		there a	bus to the airport?
	Are		there any	taxis?

C ▶ 6.4 Listen and check.

D ▶ 6.5 **LINKING** Listen again and repeat. Pay attention to the linking words.

There's⌣a … There⌣are some … There⌣are⌣a lot⌣of …
There⌣isn't⌣an … There⌣aren't⌣any … Is there⌣a …
Are there⌣any …

▷ page 128 **LANGUAGEBANK**

speakout TIP

When one word finishes with a consonant sound and the next word starts with a vowel sound, the two words join and sound like one word. Mark the links in these phrases:
How much is it? When does it leave?

4 A Underline the correct alternative.

1 There's *a/an* airport.
2 There are *some/any* stations.
3 There aren't *a lot/any* taxis.
4 There are *a lot/some* of motorbikes.
5 There isn't *a/an* underground.
6 There are *any/some* buses at night.
7 There aren't *some/any* problems with cars in the centre.
8 There are *any/a lot of* bikes.

B Work alone. Make the sentences true for your hometown/city or a town/city you know.

C Work in pairs and take turns to ask questions. Student A: you are a visitor to the town/city.

A: Is there an airport?
B: Yes, there are two airports. One is for international flights and one is for national flights.

SPEAKING

5 A Work in pairs. Student A: turn to page 152. Student B: ask questions to complete the information for Sydney and London.

B: Is there a train from the airport to Sydney?
A: Yes, there is. It's fifteen dollars.

	Sydney	London (Heathrow)
train / from the airport?		
underground?		
airport bus?		
other information?		

B Change roles. Answer Student A's questions about Barcelona and Hong Kong.

A: Is there a train from the airport to Barcelona?
B: Yes, there is. It's four euros.

	Barcelona	Hong Kong
train / from the airport?	€4	HK$100
underground?	yes but not from the airport	no
airport bus?	€6	HK$40
other information?	taxi, €30	taxi HK$300

C What's the best way to go from the airport to the centre in these four cities?

F buying a ticket
P word stress for checking
V travel

VOCABULARY

TRAVEL

1 A Work in pairs. For a long journey do you prefer bus, train, car or plane? Why?

B Look at the words in the box. Which things can you see in the photos?

> a passenger   a ticket machine   a gate
> a single (ticket)   a return (ticket)   a bus station
> a monthly pass   a platform

C Work in pairs. Which words in the box above are <u>not</u> for travel by plane?

2 A Put the actions in order.

a) Get on the bus
b) Buy a return ticket
c) Go to the ticket machine *1*
d) Show your ticket
e) Wait for the bus
f) Go to the gate
g) Get off the bus

B Work in pairs. Cover Exercise 2A and take turns to describe the actions. Use linkers.

A: First you go to the ticket machine.
B: Then you …
A: After that you …

FUNCTION

BUYING A TICKET

3 ▶ 6.6 Listen to the conversation at a bus station and tick the correct answer.

1 She wants:
   a) a single   **b) a return** ✓   c) two returns
2 She wants a ticket for:
   a) today   b) tomorrow   **c) today and tomorrow** ✓
3 It costs:
   a) €25   **b) €29** ✓   c) €39
4 It leaves at:
   a) 2.30   b) 2.15   c) 3.30
5 It arrives at:
   a) 3.15   **b) 4.15**   c) 4.45

4 A ▶ 6.7 Complete the conversation. Then listen and check.

A: A ticket ¹ _to_ Amsterdam, please.
B: ² _Single_ or return?
A: A return, please.
B: Leaving today?
A: Yes.
B: When do you want to ³ _come_ back?
A: Tomorrow afternoon.
B: OK. That's twenty-nine euros.
A: Sorry? How ⁴ _much_?
B: Twenty-nine euros.
A: What time's the ⁵ _next_ bus?
B: There's one at half past two.
A: Right. What time ⁶ _does_ it arrive in Amsterdam?
B: At quarter past four. Here's your ticket.
A: Thank you. ⁷ _Which_ gate is it?
B: The bus ⁸ _leaves_ from gate twenty-four.

B Listen again and say the sentences at the same time.

C Work in pairs and take turns. Practise the conversation.

D Write ten key words to help you remember the conversation. Then practise again.

▷ page 128 **LANGUAGEBANK**

LEARN TO

CHECK NUMBERS

5 A ▶ **6.8** WORD STRESS FOR CHECKING Listen and underline the stressed syllable in the numbers.

B: The bus leaves from gate twenty-four.
A: Sorry? Gate thirty-four?
B: No, gate twenty-four.
A: Thanks a lot.

B Listen again and repeat.

speakout TIP

Use stress to check and correct numbers.
Sorry, fifty-<u>five</u>? No, fifty-<u>nine</u>.

C Work in pairs and take turns. Practise the conversations.

1 **A:** That's 250 euros.
  B: Sorry? 240?
  A: No, 250.
2 **B:** It's bus number 72.
  A: Sorry? 72?
  B: Yes, that's right. 72.
3 **A:** The train leaves at 5 o'clock.
  B: Sorry? 9 o'clock?
  A: No, 5 o'clock.

6 A Write down three prices, three train times and three bus numbers. Don't show your partner.

B Work in pairs and take turns. Student A: read your numbers fast. Student B: repeat the numbers to check.

A: Two dollars and forty cents.
B: Sorry? Ten dollars and forty cents?
A: No, <u>two</u> dollars and forty cents.

SPEAKING

7 A Work in pairs. Student A: look at the information below. Student B: turn to page 153.

Student A: you are at the central bus station in Bogotá, Colombia. It's 8.30a.m. You want to buy a ticket to Medellin. Ask Student B questions to complete your notes.

ticket:	*a single to Medellin*
price:	
time of first bus:	
arrival time:	
gate:	

B Change roles. Student A: you work in a ticket office in the central train station in Istanbul, Turkey. Look at the information and answer Student B's questions.

>>>>> ISTANBUL TO SOFIA TRAIN SERVICE <<<<<

TICKET PRICES	
Single	90 lira
Return	170 lira
TIMES	
Departure	10.00p.m.
Arrival	10.50a.m.
Platform	6

>>>>> ISTANBUL TO SOFIA TRAIN SERVICE <<<<<

DVD PREVIEW

1 A What do you know about India? Write the correct answer a)–h) next to each sentence 1–7.

1 These are both Indian food. *a)*
2 It's a big city, but not the capital. *d*
3 It's the capital. *b*
4 She's famous for her work in India.
5 He's a famous Indian. *c*
6 It's a famous river. *f*
7 It's a beautiful building. *h*

a) daal
b) Delhi
c) Mahatma Gandhi
d) Mumbai
e) naan
f) the Ganges
g) Mother Teresa
h) the Taj Mahal

B Read the programme information and look at the photos. How do people go to work and school in India?

►)) Visions Of India: Rush Hour

BBC

Each programme in the BBC's Visions Of India shows a different side of this country of one billion people. This programme looks at how millions of working Indians travel to work and school every day.

DVD VIEW

2 A Watch the DVD and check your ideas in Exercise 1B.

B Complete the sentences with the adjectives in the box below.

popular   crowded   slow   dangerous   noisy   expensive

1 A lot of people like it. It's ____popular____.
2 It isn't quiet. It's __noisy__.
3 It costs a lot. It's __expensive__
4 It isn't safe. It's __dangerous__
5 It has a lot of people. It's __crowded__.
6 It isn't fast. It's __slow__.

C Watch the DVD again and underline the adjectives you hear for each type of transport.

1 trains – <u>crowded</u>, popular, noisy
2 bikes – dangerous, fast, slow
3 motorbikes – fast, noisy, dangerous
4 tuk-tuks – popular, fast, noisy
5 taxis – fast, safe, expensive

D Work in pairs and complete the sentences from the DVD with types of transport. Then watch the DVD again and check your answers.

1 I like it because I can see a lot of places and people from the __divan__
2 I live in Delhi, and I go to work by __buek__ every day.
3 There are sometimes bad accidents with lorries and __motbak__
4 __Takaket__ are very popular, but they are also very noisy.
5 I travel to Mumbai on business a lot. In Mumbai I usually travel by __taxis__

speakout a travel survey

3 A Work in pairs and discuss. How do people in your country travel in cities and in the countryside? How do they travel to work/to school/to the shops/on holiday?

B ▶ 6.9 Listen to a student describe how people travel in his country and complete the table.

in a big city	in the countryside
1 *by car*	1 by car
2 by underground	2 by bus
3 by bus	3 by bike
4 by train	
5 by bike	

C Listen again and tick the key phrases you hear.

> **KEY PHRASES**
>
> I live in [São Paulo] but I'm from [the countryside/…].
> There's a good public transport system.
> [A lot of/Some people] use [the underground/buses/…].
> Some people go to work by [bus/bike/…].
> The best way to travel is by [car/underground/…].
> People also go by [bus/…].
> In [my village/the city], I go everywhere by [car/bike/…].

4 A Work with a new partner and talk about the different ways people travel in your country. Use the key phrases to help.

B Work in groups and tell other students.

writeback a travel forum entry

5 A A travel website asks people to write about transport in their town/city. Read the forum entry. How does the writer usually travel?

> I live in Kobe, Japan and I work in Osaka. I think the best way to travel is by train. I go by the JR train line every morning. There are sometimes ten trains every hour. It's about thirty minutes from Kobe to Osaka. I have a monthly pass but I think a single ticket is about 500 yen.
>
> In Kobe, people travel by car, but there's a good public transport system, so a lot of people use buses and the underground. A one-day tourist pass is 1,000 yen. I live near the centre so I usually walk everywhere. Kobe is a small city, and it's a good city for walkers.

B Which things does the writer write about?
- the best way to travel ✓
- the number of trains, buses or underground trains
- the travel time
- the cost of travel
- cycling
- walking

C Write about transport in your town/city or a town/city you know for the travel website. Write 80–100 words. Use the prompts in Exercise 5B to help.

Ⓥ PLACES

1 A Add the vowels to the places.

1. i n t e r n e t c a f é
2. r _a_ st _a_ _u_ r _a_ nt
3. ph _a_ rm _a_ cy
4. n _e_ ws _a_ g _e_ nt's
5. p _a_ yph _o_ n _e_
6. c _a_ sh m _a_ ch _i_ n _e_
7. h _o_ t _i_ l
8. c _a_ f _e_

B Work in pairs. Write two things or activities connected to the places above.

internet café – a website, write emails

C Work in groups. Student A: say your things or activities. Other students: guess the place.

A: *a website, write emails*
B: *An internet café.*
A: *That's right.*

car

Ⓖ THERE IS/ARE

2 A Complete the questions asked in a hotel with *Is there* or *Are there*.

1. _____Is there_____ a swimming pool?
2. _is there_ a restaurant in the hotel?
3. _Aer there_ two beds in my room?
4. _is there_ a guided tour of the city tomorrow?
5. _Aer there_ any cash machines near the hotel?
6. _Aer there_ any other hotels near here?

B Match answers a)–f) with the questions above.

a) No, _4_, but the city isn't very interesting.
b) Yes, _6_, but they're all full.
c) Yes, _1_, but the water is very cold.
d) Yes, _2_, but it's closed now. It's open for dinner.
e) No, _3_. _____ only one bed.
f) No, _5_, but _____ one in the hotel.

C Complete the answers above with *there is/'s, there are, there isn't* or *there aren't*.

Ⓥ TRANSPORT

3 A Circle eight transport words.

Q	P	B	H	I	U	M
B	U	S	F	H	N	O
I	A	S	N	B	D	T
K	P	L	A	N	E	O
E	E	G	J	T	R	R
K	Z	Y	G	Z	G	B
E	O	K	R	E	R	I
T	R	A	E	N	O	K
A	T	R	C	U	U	E
X	T	R	A	I	N	H
I	W	S	R	S	D	K

B Work in groups and take turns. Student A: draw, mime or describe one of the things in Exercise 3A. Other students: guess what it is.

A: *It has four wheels. A lot of passengers sit on it.*
B: *A bus?*
A: *Yes!*

Ⓖ A/AN, SOME, A LOT OF, NOT ANY

4 A Find and correct the mistakes in the sentences.

In this book:
of
1. A lot/pages don't have photos.
2. Some page _s_ have six photos.
3. There's an~~ ~~ Spanish word on page 6. *a*
4. There aren't ~~some~~ shoe on page 32. *any*
5. There isn't~~ ~~ any clocks on page 45. *aren't*
6. There's apple on page 54. *an*

B Work in pairs. Which sentences above are true? Change the others to make them true.

C Work in pairs. Write four more sentences about the book, but only one true sentence. Use *a/an, some, a lot of* and *not any*.

D Work in groups and take turns to read out your sentences. Which sentences are true?

Ⓥ TRAVEL

5 Complete the words.

1. You buy a ticket at the ticket office or at a ticket ma_chin_
2. The information window is usually in the bus st_ation_
3. The people on the bus are pa_ssengers_
4. The bus leaves from a ga_te_ .
5. The train leaves from a pl_atform_
6. A ticket from A to B is a si_ngle_
7. A ticket from A to B to A is a re_turn_
8. A ticket for four weeks is a mo_nthly_ pass.

Ⓕ BUYING A TICKET

6 A Add words to make a conversation.

A: [1]single / Lisbon, / please.
A single to Lisbon, please.
B: For when?
A: [2]I / want / go / tomorrow morning.
B: OK. That's €39.
A: [3]What time / be / first bus?
B: There's one at 10.40.
A: [4]What time / it / arrive / Lisbon?
B: At 12.15 .
A: [5]Which gate / be / it?
B: It leaves from gate 34.
A: [6]Thanks / lot.

B Work in pairs and practise the conversation.

C Work alone and change the numbers in the conversation.

D Work with a new partner and take turns to practise the new conversation. Student A: write the cost, times and gate number. Check any numbers you don't understand.

B: *OK. That's 52 euros.*
A: *Sorry? 62?*
B: *No, 52.*

READING AND GRAMMAR

1 Work in pairs and discuss. When you have a problem, do you:

- talk to family or friends about it?
- phone or email a lot of people?
- look on the internet for advice?
- think about it alone?

2 Read the text. Match the answers below with problems 1–3.

a) How about bikes? Try a cycling holiday.
b) It's important to sit down and talk.
c) Change your job!

3 A Put the words in the correct order to make questions about the three people.

1 a) Jon / breakfast / Does / have?
Does Jon have breakfast?
b) evenings / go / in / Does / he / out / the?

2 a) buy / the / Layla / food / Does?
b) her / home / husband / What / at / does / do?

3 a) there / planes / Is / problem / a / with?
b) does / on / holiday / Rob / When / go?

B Match answers 1–6 with questions 1a)–3b) above.

1 No, not often. *1b*
2 Yes, she does.
3 Yes, there is.
4 No, he doesn't, but he has lunch.
5 Nothing.
6 He doesn't. He always stays at home.

QUICK**ANSWERS**

Tell us your problem and get a quick answer

Jon's problem

My problem is I'm always tired. I work in a café from seven in the morning to six in the evening. I drink a lot of coffee at work because I'm tired. I never have breakfast but I usually have a sandwich and a cake for lunch. I don't often go out in the evenings because I'm tired.

Layla's problem

My husband does nothing in the house. I often get home after work and there isn't any food in the flat so I always buy food and cook. He says he isn't hungry and he doesn't want a big dinner. He wants to sit down and he watches TV all evening. I think it's important to have dinner together and talk.

Rob's problem

There are a lot of beautiful places in the world but I never see them. My problem is I don't like travelling by plane, train, boat or car so I never go on holiday.

LISTENING AND GRAMMAR

3 A ▶ C3.1 Listen and match conversations 1–5 with the places in the box. You do not need to use one of the places.

café *1* pharmacy cash machine newsagent's payphone internet café

B Listen again and underline the correct alternative.

	What's the problem?	What happens?
1	The coffee isn't *hot*/good.	She gets *a tea/another coffee*.
2	The shop *never has/doesn't have* the New York Times.	He *buys/doesn't buy* another paper.
3	The cash machine *doesn't have money/is broken*.	*She/Salvatore* has some money.
4	Computer number *three/five* is broken.	He *goes to another computer/ leaves*.
5	He's *cold/ill*.	He *buys/doesn't buy* something for it.

SPEAKING

4 A Work in pairs. Look at the audio script on page 157. Choose one of the conversations and practise it.

B Write six to eight keywords to help you remember the conversations.

A:
Excuse
problem, coffee, cold

B:
Yeah
Sorry, let me …

C Role-play the situation. Use the keywords to help.

5 A Work in pairs. Choose a place from Exercise 3A and a new problem. Answer the questions.

1 Where are you?
2 Who are you?
3 What's the problem?

1 newsagent's
2 customer and shop assistant
3 I want a newspaper and I only have a €20 note.

B Role-play a conversation between the two people in the place.

C Work in groups and take turns to listen to other students' conversations. Where are they? What's the problem?

SOUNDS: /ð/ AND /θ/

6 A ▶ C3.2 Listen to the sounds words. Then listen and repeat.

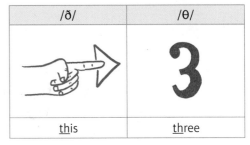

/ð/	/θ/
this	three

B ▶ C3.3 Listen and put the words in the box in the correct group. Then listen again and repeat.

thanks that monthly thirsty father with think these together thirteen

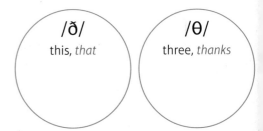

/ð/	/θ/
this, *that*	three, *thanks*

7 A ▶ C3.4 Listen and circle the correct pronunciation, a) or b).

1 together   a)   b)
2 think   a)   b)
3 these   a)   b)
4 thirsty   a)   b)
5 father   a)   b)
6 the   a)   b)
7 thank you   a)   b)
8 three   a)   b)
9 brother   a)   b)
10 month   a)   b)

B Work in pairs and take turns. Say the sentences slowly.

1 These three brothers are dirty and thirsty.
2 They say thanks for the time together.
3 There are three big airports in South Africa.

C Work in pairs. Say each sentence at the same time. Speak fast.

7 past

BBC
INTERVIEWS

◗)) Where were you on
your last birthday?

7.1)) WHERE WERE YOU?

G past simple: *was/were*
P weak and strong forms: *was/were*
V dates

LISTENING

1 A Work in pairs and look at the photo. What time of year is it? What do you usually do at this time of year?

B ▶ 7.1 Listen to people talk about New Year 2000. Match the speakers with the places.

Speaker 1   at a concert
Speaker 2   at home
Speaker 3   at work
Speaker 4   in hospital
Speaker 5   on a beach

C Listen again. Who talks about …

a) family? *1*   **d)** music?   **g)** money?
b) friends?   **e)** a sunrise?   **h)** hospital?
c) fireworks? *1*   **f)** a party? *1*

GRAMMAR

PAST SIMPLE: *WAS/WERE*

2 A Underline the correct alternative in these sentences about New Year 2000.

1 I *am/was* at home. There *is/was* a family party.
2 We *are/were* in Miami.
3 We *aren't/weren't* alone.
4 *Was/Were* the party for me?

B Complete the tables with *was, wasn't, were* or *weren't.*

I/He/She/It	(+) ___was___	at home.
	(–) _____	at work.
You/We/They	(+) _____	tired.
	(–) _____	

Was	he	here?
_____	you	in class?
Yes,	he	_____.
	we	were.
No,	he	_____.
	we	_____.

3 A ▶ 7.2 Listen to the sentences and mark the stress.

1 I was at home.
2 We were tired.
3 She was at work.
4 They were here.
5 He wasn't well.
6 You weren't in class.

B WEAK AND STRONG FORMS: *was/were* Listen again to the pronunciation of *was* /wəz/, *were* /wə/, *wasn't* /wɒznt/ and *weren't* /wɜːnt/. Which are weak (unstressed)? Which are strong (stressed)? Listen again and repeat.

▷ page 130 **LANGUAGEBANK**

4 A Underline the correct alternatives.

1 Where *was/were* you last New Year? *Was/Were* you alone or with friends?
2 *Was/Were* you and your friends at a concert last New Year?
3 *Was/Were* there a party on your last birthday? Where *was/were* it? *Was/Were* your friends at the party?
4 What *was/were* the last public holiday in your country? Where *was/were* you? Who *was/were* there?

B Complete the answers to questions 1–4 above. Use *was, wasn't, were* or *weren't.*

a) I ___was___ on a mountain in Slovakia. I _____ alone – there _____ twenty friends with me.
b) No, we _____. We _____ at a party on a boat on the Amazon River.
c) Yes, there _____, but it _____ a big party because my flat's very small.
d) Our last public holiday _____ Thanksgiving. We _____ at my brother's house. My parents _____ there because they _____ on holiday in Jamaica.

C Work in pairs and take turns. Ask and answer questions 1–4 from Exercise 4A.

A: Where were you at New Year?
B: I was in Lima, Peru.
A: Were you alone?
B: No, I wasn't. I was at a party with people from work. What about you?

speakout TIP

Three questions are very useful to help you to have a good conversation: *What about you? How about you? And you?* Write these questions in your phrasebook.

VOCABULARY

DATES

5 A Number the months in order.

September ____	June ____	February ____
March ____	December ____	October ____
January _1_	July ____	August ____
May ____	November ____	April ____

B ▶ 7.3 Listen and check. Then listen and repeat.

C Work in pairs and take turns. Student A: say a month. Student B: say the next month.

A: May
B: June

6 A Write the numbers.

1 fifth	_5th_	**7** thirty-first	_____
2 second	_2nd_	**8** eighth	_____
3 ninth	_____	**9** first	_____
4 twentieth	_____	**10** twenty-second	_____
5 fourth	_____	**11** fifteenth	_____
6 third	_____	**12** twelfth	_____

B ▶ 7.4 Listen and number the dates in the order you hear them.

15th October ____	8th August ____
1st December _1_	21st September ____
16th April ____	25th March ____

C Listen again and repeat the dates.

the first of December

7 A Work in pairs. Write three important dates in your life or in your country. Student A: say the dates. Student B: write the dates down.

B Ask each other about the dates.

B: Why is the nineteenth of March important?
A: It's my birthday.

▷ page 145 **PHOTOBANK**

SPEAKING

8 A It is Monday at 9a.m. Number the past time phrases in order.

a) last Friday ____
b) last month ____
c) yesterday evening _1_
d) this time last year ____
e) on Saturday afternoon ____

B Work in pairs and take turns. Ask about the times in Exercise 8A.

A: Where were you last Friday?
B: I was at home.

WRITING

PUNCTUATION REVIEW

9 A Match 1–5 with punctuation marks a)–e).

1 comma		**a)** !
2 full stop		**b)** .
3 exclamation mark		**c)** ?
4 question mark		**d)** A
5 capital letter		**e)** ,

B Read the email. Where's Jane? Where's Paola?

✉ 🔍 👤

Date 28/7/2012

Hi paola ¹___

How are you ²___ I'm fine and I'm in *****
with matt ³___ We're on holiday here ⁴___
Yesterday we were at the opening of the
olympic games ⁵___ Was it on television
in italy ⁶___ It was great ⁷___ There
was dancing ⁸___ singing and fantastic
fireworks ⁹___

Here's a photo ¹⁰___

Write soon ¹¹___

Best wishes ¹²___

jane

C Complete 1–12 in the email with punctuation marks. Then change six letters to capital letters.

10 A Write an email from a special place and a special time. Write three things about the place but don't write the name of the place.

B Work in groups and read other students' emails. Guess the place.

G past simple: regular verbs
P -ed endings
V actions

VOCABULARY

ACTIONS

1 A ▶ 7.5 Listen and write the number next to the action you hear.

stop	*3*	arrive	*5*
start	*1*	travel	*7*
walk	*10*	try	*9*
play tennis	*8*	talk	*4*
move home	*2*	wait	*6*

B Work in pairs. Student A: act or draw one of the verbs. Student B: say the verb.

READING

2 A Look at the photos. Where are the people and/or the places?

B Read the text and write the headings in the correct place.

Nonstop tennis match
Woman walks for eleven years
Man talks for six days
Grandmother sails round world

C Read the article again and write the names.

1 She moved twenty-four times.
Ffyona Campbell
2 She tried it three times. *Jeanne Socrates*
3 People listened to him. *Arvind Mishra*
4 He played tennis with Daniel. *Carlo (santel)*
5 She didn't stop. *Jeann Socrates(s)*
6 He waited. *audience member at Arvind Mishra's talk*
7 They were very happy but tired. *Carlo and Paniel*
8 She was in Africa. *Ffyona Campbell*

D Read the article again and correct the mistakes in the notes below.

talking: 139 hours, 24 minutes, 59 seconds

sailing: 295 days

playing tennis: 32 hours, 12 minutes, 9 seconds

walking: 32,000 metres

1 Man talks for six days

Arvind Mishra of Dehradun, India talked about scientific computations for 139 hours, forty-two minutes and fifty-six seconds from 1st to 6th March, 2014. One audience member said, 'I listened for thirteen hours and waited for the end, but Professor Mishra didn't stop!' After six days Mishra finally stopped, and now he has the world record!

GRAMMAR

PAST SIMPLE: REGULAR VERBS

3 A Read the article again and find the past form of the verbs below.

1 start	*started*	**4** play	*Played*	**7** try	*tried*	**10** finish *Finis*
2 talk	*talked*	**5** wait	*Waited*	**8** stop	*stopped*	**11** want *wante*
3 arrive	*arrived*	**6** move	*moved*	**9** travel	*travelled*	**12** ask *asked*

B Complete the table.

RULES

To make the past simple with regular verbs:		
sailed nonstop	**spelling**	**examples**
most verbs	add ___*ed*___	*started* *played*
verbs ending in -e	add ___*d*___	*arrived* *moved*
verbs ending in consonant + -y	change to ___*ied*___	*tried*
verbs ending in consonant + vowel + consonant	double the final letter, then add ___*ed*___	*stopped* *travelled*

C Look at the sentences and complete the rule.
Professor Mishna didn't stop!
They didn't answer our question.

RULES

Use *didn't* + verb to make the negative of the past simple.

2 _Grandmother sails round_

At the age of seventy, Jeanne Socrates sailed round the world alone. She started her trip from Victoria Harbour in Canada, and finished on 8th July, 2013, two hundred and fifty-nine days later. She is the oldest woman to sail solo nonstop around the world. 'She tried this twice before, in 2009 and 2010,' said a friend. 'But there were some problems with the boat and she didn't finish.'

3 _Nonstop tennis match_

Carlo Santelli and Daniel Burns played tennis for thirty-eight hours, two minutes and nine seconds on 10th May 2010 in Clifton, New Jersey, USA. We asked them about the winner but they didn't answer our question. Winning wasn't important to them. They only wanted to break the world record.

4 _Woman walks for eleven years_

Ffyona Campbell travelled around the world in eleven years. The amazing thing is that she walked almost all the 32,000 kilometres. In Africa, she started in Cape Town in 1991 and arrived in Tangiers in 1993. Why did she walk so much? Well, maybe it was because of her childhood; she moved home twenty-four times before she was sixteen!

---

4 A ▶ 7.6 **-ed ENDINGS** Listen to the pronunciation of the verbs and write them in the correct place.

/t/   tal<u>ked</u>
/d/   arriv<u>ed</u>
/ɪd/ start<u>ed</u>

B ▶ 7.7 Listen and check. Then listen again and repeat.

▷ page 130 **LANGUAGEBANK**

5 A Complete the sentences with the past form of the verbs in brackets.

1 He _lived_ (live) here when he was a boy, **but** then he _moved_ (move) to the countryside.
2 We _waited_ (wait) for hours, **but** the bus _didn't arrive_ (not arrive).
3 My friend _cooked_ (cook) dinner last night **and** I really _liked_ (like) it.
4 I usually drive, but yesterday I _walked_ (walk) **because** they _closed_ (close) the road.
5 The teacher _asked_ (ask) me a question, **but** I _didn't_ (not understand).
6 I _watched_ (watch) a very sad film last night **and** I _cried_ (cry) the whole time.

B Work in pairs and take turns. Student A: close your book. Student B: read the first part of the sentences in Exercise 5A. Stop after the word in bold. Student A: try to remember the end of the sentence.

B: He lived here when he was a boy, but …
A: then he moved to the countryside.

SPEAKING

6 A Make six true sentences about yourself, the teacher and a friend in the past.

I
The teacher
* _____

+	live watch (TV/a film) stay talk walk text play (football/tennis/golf)

+	alone (with/to) my family (with/to) me (with/to) * _____

+	yesterday two days ago last weekend last year when I was young

* Write the name of a friend or student here.

B Change three of your sentences so that they are false.

C Work in groups and take turns. Student A: read one of your sentences. Other students: say if it's true or false.

A: Simon texted Lena yesterday.
B: False.
A: That's right. He didn't text Lena. He texted me.

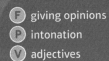

F giving opinions
P intonation
V adjectives

FUNCTION

ASKING FOR AND GIVING OPINIONS

1 A Work in pairs. Look at the pictures and discuss the questions.

Where are the people? How do they feel?

B ▶ 7.8 Listen to three conversations. Are the conversations about a film (F), a party (P) or a restaurant meal (R)? Write the letter.

1 ____   2 ____   3 ____

C Listen again. Match phrases 1–6 with a)–f).

1 It's fantastic.   a) steak
2 It was very good.   b) chicken
3 It's terrible. ←   c) Warren's party
4 It was boring.   d) ice cream
5 It wasn't very good.   e) film
6 Delicious.   f) Adam's party

2 A ▶ 7.9 Put the words in order to make questions and opinions. Then listen and check.

1 **A:** was / your / How / steak?
   How was your steak?
   B: Delicious, / right. / just
2 **A:** your / was / chicken? / How
   B: good. / It / very / wasn't
3 **A:** cream? / ice / the / of / What / think / you / do
   B: fantastic! / 's / It
4 **A:** party? / was / the / How
   B: boring. / It / was

B Underline two or three stressed words in each question or phrase above.

C Listen and check. Then listen again and repeat.

D Work in pairs and practise the conversations.

▷ page 130 **LANGUAGEBANK**

VOCABULARY

ADJECTIVES

3 A Write the adjectives in the correct group.

| all right terrible fantastic great delicious |
| not very good boring interesting awful |
| not bad |

+	–	+/–
fantastic	*terrible*	*all right*

B Work in pairs and answer the questions about the adjectives above.

1 Which four adjectives mean <u>very</u> good (VG)?
2 Which three adjectives mean <u>very</u> bad (VB)?
3 Which adjective is <u>only</u> for food (F)?
fantastic VG

C ▶ 7.10 Listen and underline the stress in the adjectives. Then listen and repeat.

all <u>right</u>

D Work in pairs and look at photos A–C. Describe the food, the party and the film.

A: *I think the food is …*

4 A Write the name of a person, place or thing for each adjective in Exercise 3A.

fantastic – Daniel Craig   boring – golf
all right – my town

B Work in pairs and take turns. Student A: say a person, place or thing on your list. Student B: guess Student A's adjective.

A: *Golf*
B: *Great?*
A: *No.*
B: *Boring?*
A: *Yes. I think golf is really boring. What about you?*

▷ page 145 **PHOTOBANK**

SPEAKING

6 A Add words to make a conversation.

Student A

> Where / you / last night?

Student B

> I / go / to the Adele concert.

> How / it?

> It / fantastic! I / love / it.

> How / be / Adele?

> She / be / great.

> Yes, she / be / very good.

> And you? Where / be / you?

> I / go / to the cinema / to see (name of film)

> How / be / it?

> It / OK but (name of actor/actress) / be / great.

A: Where were you last night?
B: I went* to the Adele concert.
*went = the past of go

B Work in pairs and take turns. Role-play the conversation.

C Work with other students. Change the conversations to talk about a restaurant, a party, a class, a different film, or a different concert.
A: Where were you last night?
B: I was at the new Chinese restaurant.
A: Oh, how was it?

7 Work with other students. Ask and answer about last weekend.
A: Where were you last weekend?
B: I was at my brother's house.

LEARN TO
SHOW FEELINGS

5 A ▶ 7.11 Listen to the questions and opinions again. Does speaker B feel positive (+) or negative (−)?

1 _____   2 _____   3 _____   4 _____

B INTONATION Listen again. Is speaker B's voice high (H) or low (L)?

 **TIP**

When you give an opinion, use high intonation for a positive feeling (*Beautiful!*) and flat or low intonation for a negative feeling (*Terrible!*)

Beautiful!   *Terrible!*

C Work in pairs and take turns. Ask and answer questions using the words below. Use high or low intonation in your answers.

How was ...	
the film?	great
the concert?	fantastic
the party?	delicious
your party?	not very good
the food?	terrible
your weekend?	awful
	very nice
	boring

A: How was your holiday?
B: It wasn't very good.

DVD PREVIEW

1 A Work in pairs and match the words in the box with pictures A–H.

> a drill *A*   a miner   a tunnel   a microphone
> a note   underground   the surface   an accident

A   B   C

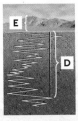

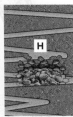

E   F   D   G   H

B Read the programme information about the Chilean miners' rescue and complete the summary.

◀)) The Chilean Miners' Rescue

BBC

In 2010 there was an accident at a mine near Copiapó, Chile. Thirty-three miners were underground at the time. Were they dead or alive? For seventeen days, their families and friends waited. Then, on Day 17, a note arrived from the mine: it was from the men. They were OK. Workers drilled down to the miners for many weeks. People around the world watched and waited. Finally after sixty-nine days, one by one, the miners travelled to the surface They were free! Watch their story on tonight's Newsround.

> In ___2010___ , _____ miners were underground
> for _____ days at a mine in Chile. For the first
> _____ days, no one knew they were alive.

DVD VIEW

2 A Watch the DVD. Was the last man out of the mine an ill miner, the oldest miner or the boss?

B Complete sentences 1–6 with words from the box below. Then watch the DVD again to check your answers.

> ~~seven~~   days   worked   families   travelled   rescue

1 Thirty-three miners were underground, ___seven___ hundred metres underground.
2 The miners _____ to keep healthy and positive.
3 The miners' _____ watched and waited.
4 The tunnel was finished. The _____ started.
5 One by one the miners _____ to the surface.
6 After sixty-nine _____, the miners were free.

C Work in pairs and look at the sentences. What does the underlined word in each sentence refer to? Then watch the DVD again or read the script and check your ideas.

1 They listened to microphones.
2 It was from the miners.
3 We are well in the shelter.
4 The world watched with them.
5 It was eighteen minutes…
6 He was the boss.

speakout do a quiz

3 A Work in pairs. Put the news events on the timeline.

a) Nelson Mandela died
b) The Japanese tsunami
c) Google started
d) The first man on the moon

1969 1975   1987   1996   2007 2011 2013

B ▶ 7.12 Listen to two people doing the task and check your answers.

C Listen again and tick the key phrases you hear.

> **KEY PHRASES**
>
> Which was first?
> I think [the Japanese tsunami] was [first/next].
> Yes, I agree.
> I don't know./I'm not sure.
> No, Google was [before/after] the Japanese tsunami.
> Which date?
> I remember it well.
> Let's check the answers.
> We were [right/wrong] about [three answers/ Google.

D Work in groups. Do the quiz on page 151. Use the key phrases to help.

writeback a history quiz

4 A Read and answer three questions from a quiz.

1 **When were the first modern Olympic Games?**
   a) 296   b) 1896   c) 1996

2 **Which US president's father was also president?**
   a) George Washington   b) George W. Bush
   c) Barack Obama

3 **Why was Evita famous?**
   a) she was a politician   b) she was a pop star
   c) she was a sportswoman

4 **What was Picasso's first name?**
   a) Pueblo   b) Pierre   c) Pablo

See answers at the bottom of the page.

B Work in pairs and write three more questions about famous people, places and events. For each question, write three answers, one true and two false. Use the questions in Exercise 4A and the prompts below to help.

When was/were … ? Who was/were … ?
Where was/were … ? What was/were … ?
Which (king, queen, president, country, etc.) was … ?

C Work with a new partner and take turns. Ask and answer your questions. Use the key phrases to help.

Ⓖ PAST SIMPLE: WAS/WERE

1 A Write the questions for 1–8. Find someone who …

1 was very happy yesterday.
Were you very happy yesterday?
2 was tired this morning.
3 was in the town/city centre at the weekend.
4 was here in the last class.
5 was in a café before class.
6 was on a train at eight o'clock this morning.
7 was late for something yesterday.
8 was ill yesterday.

B Work in groups and ask the questions. If a student says *yes*, write his/her name.

A: *Were you very happy yesterday?*
B: *Yes, I was. It was my birthday.*

Ⓥ DATES

2 A Write today's date.

_____

B Write the dates for the time phrases below.

1 yesterday

_____

2 last year

_____

3 last month

_____

4 last Saturday

_____

5 last Tuesday

_____

6 last night

_____

C Work in pairs. Student A: say a time phrase from Exercise 2B. Student B: say the date.

D Write a different date and repeat Exercise 2C.

Wednesday, 11th March 20[year]
A: *Yesterday.*
B: *Tuesday 10th March 20[year].*
A: *Last year.*
B: *20[year].*

Ⓥ ACTIONS

3 A Put the letters in the correct order to make actions. Start with the underlined letter.

1 t<u>wi</u>a *wait*   6 vert<u>a</u>l
2 k<u>t</u>la   7 ratt<u>s</u>
3 yr<u>t</u>   8 kla<u>w</u>
4 veri<u>a</u>r   9 ve<u>m</u>o he<u>m</u>o
5 p<u>s</u>ot   10 yal<u>p</u> sen<u>ti</u>n

B Complete the sentences with one of the actions above.

1 We _move home_ every year.
2 I never _____ late for lessons.
3 My day _____ at 6a.m.
4 The teacher sometimes _____ too fast.
5 Sometimes I _____ to work, sometimes I drive.
6 I usually _____ by car in the city.
7 I always _____ new food in restaurants.
8 I never _____ when someone is late for a meeting.
9 I don't often _____ but I watch matches on TV.
10 I often _____ and look at my watch.

C Work in pairs. Which of the sentences in Exercise 3B are true for you? Change the other sentences to make them true.

Ⓖ PAST SIMPLE: REGULAR VERBS

4 A Change the verbs to the past form.

1 watch_ed_ a film on a plane
2 wait_____ for a bus
3 phone_____ someone
4 ask_____ a question on the internet
5 play_____ with a child
6 study_____ English grammar
7 stop_____ someone on the street
8 try_____ something new

B Work in pairs. Ask and answer questions with the phrases above. Start your question: *When was the last time you …?*

A: *When was the last time you watched a film on a plane?*
B: *Last year. I was on a plane from Madrid to Berlin. The film was …*

Ⓥ ADJECTIVES

5 A Add the vowels to the adjectives.

1 t__rr__bl__
2 d__l__c_____s
3 __nt__r__st__ng
4 __wf__l
5 f__nt__st__c
6 b__r__ng
7 gr____t
8 __ll r__ght
9 n__t v__ry g____d
10 n__t b__d

B Work in pairs and make short conversations. Use the adjectives above and words in the box.

the film   the food   the match
the concert   the lesson

A: *The concert was terrible!*
B: *Yes, it was awful.*

Ⓕ ASKING FOR AND GIVING OPINIONS

6 A Put the sentences in order to make a conversation.

B: Because the food was terrible. And how was the film?
B: He's not bad.
B: It wasn't very good. *2*
A: Yes, I think he's all right too.
A: Why not?
A: It was great, really good. Hey, what do you think of our new manager?
A: Hi, Pete, how was the restaurant last night? *1*

B Work in pairs and practise the conversation.

8)) places

ANGE MEETINGS p84   A GOOD HOLIDAY? p86   WHERE IS IT? p88   GUIDED TOUR p90

SPEAKING   **8.1** Talk about first meetings   **8.2** Ask and answer about a good holiday
                  8.3 Give directions in a supermarket   **8.4** Tell a bad holiday story

LISTENING   **8.2** Listen to a radio programme about holidays   **8.3** Listen to someone asking for
                  directions in a supermarket   **8.4** Watch a BBC comedy about tourists in Spain

READING   **8.1** Read about how people met their friends

WRITING   **8.1** Use linkers *so* and *because*   **8.4** Write a travel review

BBC INTERVIEWS

)) Where did you go
on holiday last year?

G past simple: irregular verbs
P sounds: irregular past verbs
V prepositions of place

READING

1 A Work in pairs and answer the questions.

1 Where do people usually meet new people?

2 Look at the photos. Where are the places? Are they places where you usually meet new friends?

B Read the text. Which story is really unusual?

C Underline the mistake in each sentence. Try to remember the correct information from the text.

1 The bus was in the mountains.

2 Habib was the bus driver.

3 The bridge was in India.

4 Cynthia and Anne were on the bridge for an hour.

5 Jon was in a train accident.

6 Jon was in hospital for a month.

7 Someone took Alison's passport.

8 The waitress said, 'Do you need money?'

D Read the text again and check your answers.

GRAMMAR

PAST SIMPLE: IRREGULAR VERBS

2 A Write the past forms of the verbs. Use the text in Exercise 1B to help. Check any new words.

1	meet	_met_	**6** break	_____
2	come	_____	**7** go	_____
3	take	_____	**8** have	_____
4	think	_____	**9** sit	_____
5	become	_____	**10** say	_____

B ▶ 8.1 Listen and check. Then listen and repeat.

speakout TIP

When you learn a new verb, check your dictionary and write the past form in your phrasebook, e.g. *go – went*. Do this with these verbs: *drive, eat, see, give, put.*

C ▶ 8.2 **SOUNDS: irregular past verbs** Write the irregular past verbs from Exercise 2A and the Speakout tip next to the correct sound. Then listen and check.

1 /e/ _met_, _____, _____, _____

2 /eɪ/ _came_, _____, _____

3 /ʊ/ _took_, _____

4 /æ/ _had_, _____

5 /əʊ/ _broke_, _____

6 /ɔː/ _thought_, _____

D Underline the correct alternative to make the negative. Use the text to help.

I *didn't have/didn't had* any money.

▷ page 132 **LANGUAGEBANK**

What a strange place to meet!

Tell us where you met your best friend and win a holiday for two.

In Algeria, in the Sahara desert. I was on a bus to Timimoun, a town in the desert. The bus had engine problems and we stopped in a small village for the night. The local people were very friendly, and one guy, Habib, took me home to his family. I thought he was a really nice person. We talked a lot and became great friends.

Omar

In hospital in China. I was in a car accident and broke my leg. I went to hospital and was there for a week. There was a Chinese guy in my room, Li. We had a lot of time to talk and became great friends.

Jon

In a café in Argentina. I was on holiday and someone took my money. I sat down in a café. I didn't have any money but I was very hungry. The waitress came to my table and said, 'Hi, I'm Claudia. Do you need help?' We were instant best friends!

Alison

On a rope bridge in Pakistan! I walked from one side, and another woman, Anne, walked from the other side. We met in the centre, and we were both very scared. We were there for half an hour. Finally, a guide came and helped us. After that half-hour together we were friends for life.

Cynthia

3 A Read the stories. Who are the people?

1 In about 2005, I ^{1} _was_ (be) at a shop in my village and a man ^{2} _____ (come) in, a tourist. He ^{3} _____ (not want) anything at the shop, but he ^{4} _____ (ask) about a hotel. I ^{5} _____ (drive) him to my house and he ^{6} _____ (meet) my family, and ^{7} _____ (stay) with us for the night. I ^{8} _____ (think) he was a great guy and later we ^{9} _____ (become) good friends.

2 In 2012, I ^{1} _____ (work) as a waitress at a café. One day I was at work and I ^{2} _____ (see) a woman alone and very unhappy. I ^{3} _____ (go) over to her and ^{4} _____ (say), 'Hi, do you need help?' She ^{5} _____ (not have) any money and she ^{6} _____ (not know) anyone in the city. I ^{7} _____ (sit) down and ^{8} _____ (talk) to her. Then I ^{9} _____ (give) her some money and food. Now she's one of my best friends.

B Complete the stories with the past forms of the verbs in brackets.

C Work in pairs. Student A: change three things in story 1. Student B: change three things in story 2.

café
In about 2005, I was at a ~~shop~~ in my village and …

D Work in pairs and take turns. Student A: read your story. Student B: listen to Student A and stop the story when you hear something different.

A: I was at a café in my village.
B: Stop! No, you were in a shop in your village.

VOCABULARY

PREPOSITIONS OF PLACE

4 A Underline the correct alternative.

1 We were *at/in/on* a bridge.

2 We met *at/in/on* China.

3 I was *at/in/on* work.

B Complete the word webs with *in, on* or *at*.

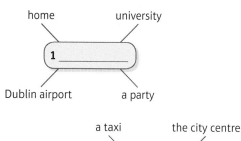

home   university

1 _____

Dublin airport   a party

a taxi   the city centre

2 _____

class   Rome

holiday   a chair

3 _____

the internet   television

5 A Complete the sentences with *in, on* or *at*.

at
1 I met my best friend / school.

2 I met one of my friends the internet.

3 I went holiday with a friend last year.

4 I wasn't class last week.

5 I was a friend's party on Saturday.

6 I had lunch with a friend the city centre yesterday.

B Tick the sentences that are true for you. Change the other sentences to make them true for you.

▷ page 146 **PHOTOBANK**

SPEAKING

6 A Write the name of three friends on the timeline. Write the year and place you met.

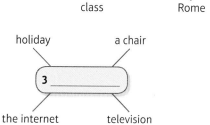

Viki

2005 university   Now

B Work in groups and take turns. Show your timeline and talk about your friends. Other students: ask questions.

A: Viki is a good friend. We met in 2005 at university.
B: Were you students? Where exactly did you meet? Why did you like her? Where is she now?

8.2)) A GOOD HOLIDAY?

G past simple: questions
P linking: *did you?*
V holiday activities

VOCABULARY

HOLIDAY ACTIVITIES

1 A Work in pairs. When was the last time you went on holiday? Was it a good holiday? Why?/Why not?

B Match verbs 1–4 with a)–d) and verbs 5–8 with e)–h).

1 see	**a)** the local water
2 eat	**b)** ill
3 drink	**c)** old buildings
4 become	**d)** the local food
5 go	**e)** English
6 meet	**f)** a good time
7 speak	**g)** camping
8 have	**h)** the local people

C Work in pairs. Which activities above are in the pictures?

D Work in pairs and take turns. Student A: say the ending. Student B: say the activity.

A: old buildings
B: See old buildings.

E Work in pairs and take turns to ask and answer. Which activities do you do when you're on holiday?

A: On holiday, do you usually drink the local water?
B: Yes, I do, but I sometimes drink mineral water. How about you?

LISTENING

2 A Work alone. Look at the photos and number the holidays a)–e) in order (1–5). 1 = My favourite type of holiday, 5 = I don't like this type of holiday.

a) a camping holiday with your family ___
b) a beach holiday with a friend in Surfer's Paradise, Australia ___
c) a group sightseeing weekend in Paris, France ___
d) two months in China alone ___
e) a walking holiday in Peru with a friend ___

B Work in pairs and compare your answers.

A: For number one, I put a group sightseeing weekend in Paris.
B: Why?
A: I like France and Paris is beautiful. And I like group tours. What about you?

3 A ▶ 8.3 Listen to a radio programme about good and bad holidays. Write good (G) or bad (B) next to the holidays in Exercise 2A.

B Underline the correct information. Then listen again and check your ideas.

1 He went camping in <u>Canada</u>/Cambodia.
2 They didn't have *tea/television*.
3 He lost his *passport/girlfriend*.
4 He had some bad *food/water*.
5 She *got/didn't get* to Paris.
6 She ate *lunch/dinner* on the train.
7 She met *English/Chinese* people.
8 She *spoke/didn't speak* Chinese.

GRAMMAR

PAST SIMPLE: QUESTIONS

4 A ▶ 8.4 Listen and complete the table.

Questions and short answers								
?	_____	you	like	it?	Yes,	I	_____	
			speak	English?	No,		_____	
Wh - questions								
Where						go?		
What		_____		you		do?		

B LINKING: *did you?* Listen to the questions and short answers. Then listen again and repeat.

Did_you … ?
/dɪdʒʊ/

▷ page 132 **LANGUAGEBANK**

5 A Add words to make yes/no questions.

1 go / holiday / last year? *Did you go on holiday last year?*
2 have / good time?
3 meet / friends / last night?
4 speak / English / yesterday?
5 have / breakfast / morning?

B Add words to complete the answers.

1 (+ we. / go / to Greece) *Yes, we did. We went to Greece.*
2 (+ we. / have / great time. / stay / good hotel)
3 (– I. / stay / home / watch / film on TV)
4 (+ I. / speak English / my teacher)
5 (– I. / be / not hungry / and / be / late)

C Work in pairs and take turns. Ask the questions in Exercise 5A and answer about yourself.

A: *Did you go on holiday last year?*
B: *Yes, I did. I went to Bulgaria, to the Black Sea.*

▷ page 146 **PHOTOBANK**

SPEAKING

6 A Work alone. Complete the questions with a word from the box. Use the student's notes to help you.

Where (x 2)   Why   Did   What   How (x 3)

1 *Where* and when did you go? *Italy – 2015*
2 _____ you go alone or with friends or family? *friend – Dave*
3 _____ did you travel there? *by plane – 5 hours*
4 _____ did you stay? *small hotel*
5 _____ was the weather? *sunny*
6 _____ was the food? *v. good*
7 _____ did you do? *relaxed – beach*
8 _____ did you like it? *people – food – weather*

B Write notes to answer the questions in Exercise 6A about a good holiday you had.

1 Italy – in 2015 – four weeks

C Work in groups and take turns. Student A: talk about your holiday. Other students: ask questions.

WRITING

SO AND *BECAUSE*

7 A Match sentences 1–3 with a)–c).

Holiday problems

1 In Denmark, we went camping because the hotels were expensive.
2 In Hong Kong, I thought the city was dangerous so I didn't go out at night.
3 In Barcelona, we were hungry at 6p.m. so we looked for a restaurant.

a) Big mistake – I went out on the last night and it was great!
b) Big mistake – they only open at 9p.m!
c) Big mistake – it was cold at night!

B Underline *so* and *because* in sentences 1–3 above. Which word answers the question *why*?

C Underline the correct alternative.

1 We walked *so/because* there were no buses.
2 There were no buses *so/because* we walked.

D Complete the sentences in Exercise 7A in a different way.

1 In Denmark the hotels were expensive so …
2 In Hong Kong I didn't go out at night because …
3 In Barcelona we looked for a restaurant at 6p.m. because …

8 A Add *so* or *because* to the sentences.

1 Our plane was at three we got to the airport at two.
2 I didn't book a hotel I didn't have time.
3 We went to New Zealand in July we have school holidays in the summer.
4 There was no mineral water we drank the local water.

B Work in pairs. What was the 'big mistake' in situations 1–4 in Exercise 8A? Write your ideas.

1 Big mistake – the check-in closed at one so we …

C Write an email to a friend about your bad holiday. Use ideas from Exercise 8A. Write 50–70 words.

(F) giving directions
(P) word stress: prepositions
(V) prepositions of place

SPEAKING

1 Work in pairs and answer the questions.

1 Do you enjoy supermarket shopping?
2 Where did you last buy some food? What was it?
3 How many words can you remember for food?

VOCABULARY

PREPOSITIONS OF PLACE

2 A Match the prepositions in the box with pictures A–H.

| on the right of *F* on the left of in front of near |
| behind between next to opposite |

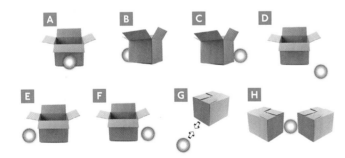

B ▶ 8.5 Listen and check.

C WORD STRESS: prepositions Listen again and match the prepositions to the stress patterns O, Oo, oO (x2), Ooo, oOo, ooOo (x2). Then listen again and repeat.

D Work in pairs and take turns. Choose a picture and ask about it.

A: Where's the ball in picture G?
B: It's opposite the box.

3 A Tick the sentences that are true for your class.

1 There are some windows next to the door.
2 The teacher usually stands behind a table.
3 I sit opposite another student.
4 There's a picture on the right of the door.
5 Our coats are near the window.
6 My bag is between my chair and the wall.

B Change the other sentences to make them true for your class.

FUNCTION

GIVING DIRECTIONS

4 A ▶ 8.6 Listen to three conversations. What does the person want to find? Write the number of the conversation next to the food.

vegetables __   bread __   fish __   fruit *1*
cereal __   cakes __   snacks __ meat __

B Listen again. Match places a)–f) below with the food. Do not use two of the places.

fruit *f*   bread __   cereal __   cakes __

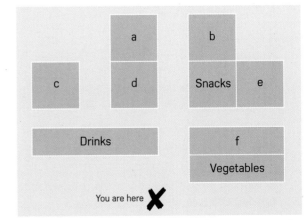

5 A Complete the conversation with the words in the in the box.

Excuse behind where see Let over of Do

A: ¹ *Excuse* me, ² _____ 's the fruit?

B: ³ _____ you ⁴ _____ the vegetables ⁵ _____ there?

A: Yes.

B: The vegetables are in front ⁶ _____ the fruit. Over there.

A: ⁷ _____ me check. The fruit's ⁸ _____ the vegetables.

B: Yes, that's right.

B Work in pairs and practise the conversation.

C Work alone. Change the names of the food and the prepositions. Then work with a new partner and role-play the new conversations.

▷ page 132 **LANGUAGEBANK**

LEARN TO

USE EXAMPLES

6 A ▷ 8.7 Listen and complete the conversations.

1 **A:** Vegetables? ¹ _____ are they?
   B: Vegetables … you ² _____, tomatoes, potatoes, carrots.
   A: Oh, vegetables.

2 **B:** Do you see the snacks?
   A: Snacks? I don't know 'snacks'.
   B: Snacks, for ³ _____, chocolate, nuts and crisps.
   A: Oh, I understand.

3 **A:** Cereal? What's ⁴ _____?
   B: Cereal. ⁵ _____ Corn Flakes.

speakout TIP

When you don't know a word, examples can help. Use the phrases *you know*, *like* and *for example* to give examples.

B Work in pairs and practise the conversations.

C Work in pairs and take turns. Student A: choose one type of food in the box and ask Student B about it. Student B: ask for an example.

meat fruit vegetables dairy

A: Where's the meat?
B: Meat? For example?
A: You know, chicken, beef, lamb.
B: Oh, meat!

SPEAKING

7 A Write the six types of food in the box in your supermarket diagram.

meat fish dairy sweets bread fruit

Your supermarket

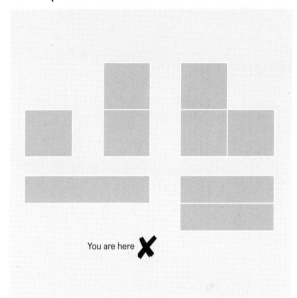

Your partner's supermarket

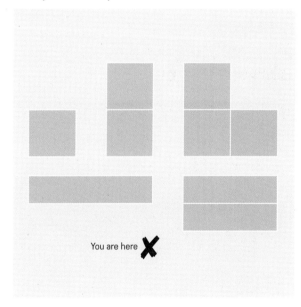

B Work in pairs and take turns to role-play the situation. Student A: you are the customer. Student B: you are a sales assistant. Ask and answer about the food in your partner's supermarket. Write the food in the correct place.

A: Excuse me. Where's the meat?
B: Do you see the … over there?
A: Yes.
B: The meat's in front of the …

DVD PREVIEW

1 A Complete the holiday questionnaire. Tick the sentences that are true for you.

On holiday, I always:

> read about the place.

> take a guided tour.

> go out in the evenings.

> take lots of photos.

B Work in pairs and compare your answers. What other things do you do on holiday?

2 Read the programme information. Are sentences 1–4 true (T) or false (F)?

1 *Little Britain* is funny.
2 A woman plays the tour guide Carol.
3 Carol is friendly.
4 This episode is in Spain.

◉⟩) Little Britain Abroad   **BBC**

The BBC comedy show, *Little Britain*, is about British people in typical situations. Carol Beer (the actor, David Walliams) is often on the show. Carol is always bored and is usually rude to people. In this episode, she is a tour guide for a group of British tourists on holiday in Majorca, Spain.

DVD VIEW

3 A Work in pairs and look at the photos. Which woman is Carol?

B Watch the DVD to check your answer.

C Watch the DVD again and number the phrases a)–g) in the order you hear them.

a) Any questions or problems, come to me ____
b) look to your right ____
c) stop the coach ____
d) Sunsearchers Holidays *1*
e) Welcome to Spain ____
f) fun, fun, fun ____
g) get out ____

D Is the information below true (T) or false (F)? Correct any false information. Then watch the clip again to check.

1 The words on the sign are very big.
F: They are very small.
2 Carol answers the couple when they say 'Good morning'.
3 The microphone is noisy.
4 Carol says 'If you look to your left, you'll see the countryside.'
5 Carol speaks good Spanish.
6 The bus driver's name is Gonzales.
7 Someone throws the couple's bags off the bus.
8 The bus waits for the couple.

E Work in groups and compare your answers to Exercise 3D. Who thought the programme was funny?

speakout a bad holiday story

4 A Work in pairs and look at the pictures. Why did the man have a bad holiday? Use the words/phrases in the box below.

bored   it rained   noisy   expensive   missed the plane

B ▶ 8.8   Listen to the man tell the story. Which picture is different from his story?

C Listen again and tick the key phrases you hear.

> **KEY PHRASES**
>
> I missed my [plane/train/bus].
> I arrived [in Honolulu] one [hour/day/week] late.
> I lost my [passport/money/bags].
> It rained for [the first three days/all week/…].
> I stayed in [my hotel room/the café/…] all day.
> The hotel was [noisy/expensive/dirty/…].
> The food was [bad/expensive/…].
> I was very happy to go home.

5 A Work in pairs and change three things about the story. Use the key phrases and practise telling your story to each other.

B Work with a new partner. Take turns to tell your stories. How many differences can you find?

writeback a travel review

6 A Read the travel review. How many positive things and how many negative things does the writer talk about?

Travel review: **Edinburgh**

◉ **Where, when, who with?**
Last year we went to Edinburgh on holiday. I went with Frieda, a friend from university.

◉ **What was good about it?**
We took a boat from Dublin to Holyhead in Wales, and then a train to Edinburgh. It was a lovely journey. We stayed at the Guthrie Hotel, near the National Gallery. It wasn't expensive and the people were friendly. Our favourite restaurant was Kings in Hanover Street. The food is fantastic there!

◉ **What was bad about it?**
Our hotel room was next to the street, so it was noisy. Also, it rained for three days non-stop, so I watched TV and read a lot of books.

◉ **What advice do you have for travellers?**
It's a good idea to bring a raincoat, and get a quiet hotel room.

B Write your own travel review for a place you know. Answer the questions in the review above. Use 80–100 words.

C Read other students' stories. Which place would you like to visit?

⑥ PAST SIMPLE: IRREGULAR VERBS

1 A Complete the sentences with the past form of the verbs.

1 I / meet / a friend in a café yesterday.

I met a friend in a café yesterday.

2 Two students / come / to class late for this lesson.

3 I / think / English was difficult, but now I think it's easy.

4 I / go / home by train last night.

5 I / not sit / here last lesson.

6 I / not have / breakfast at home.

7 I / see / the teacher in a supermarket yesterday.

B Change the sentences so they are true for you.

C Work in pairs. Student A: read your sentences. Student B: listen and say your sentence.

A: I met a friend in a restaurant yesterday.

B: I didn't meet a friend yesterday.

⑦ PREPOSITIONS OF PLACE

2 A Work in pairs. Complete the sentences with the words in the box.

> class   home   car   work
> street   bike   Rome   holiday

1 **In the morning, I have** two coffees. I have my first at _____ and my second at _____.

2 **I listen to music** in my _____, but not on my _____, because it's too dangerous.

3 **I was on** _____ in _____ last year.

4 **I like speaking English** with the teacher in _____, but not with people in the _____.

B Work alone. Write four sentences about you. Start with the words in bold in Exercise 2A and use *in*, *on* or *at*.

In the morning, I have tea at home but I drink water at work.

C Work in pairs and compare your sentences.

⑦ HOLIDAY ACTIVITIES

3 A Add vowels to complete the activities.

1 g_o_ c_a_mp_i_ng

2 sp___k __ngl_sh

3 s___ __ld b___ld_ngs

4 dr__nk th__ l_c_l w__t__r

5 ___t th__ l_c_l f____d

6 b_c_m__ __ll

7 h_v__ __ g___d t_m__

8 m___t th__ l_c_l p___pl__

B Work in pairs. Which activities above do you do:

- on a family holiday in your country with not a lot of money?
- on a weekend city break?
- in a different country?

⑥ PAST SIMPLE: QUESTIONS

4 A Find and correct the mistakes in the questions about last weekend. One question is correct.

1 Did you had a good weekend?

Did you have a good weekend?

2 What did you?

3 Met you any friends?

4 Where did you went?

5 a) Did you buy anything?

   b) What you buy?

6 a) You did see a film at the cinema or on TV?

   b) What were it?

B Work in pairs and take turns. Ask and answer the questions.

A: Did you have a good weekend?

B: Yes, great!

A: What did you do?

B: I went camping.

⑦ PREPOSITIONS

5 A Put the letters in bold in the correct order to make prepositions.

1 The tree is on the **thirg** of the shop.

2 The tree is **etenweb** the shop and the car.

3 The road is **txne** to the house.

4 The car is on the **flet** of the shop.

5 The man is **hibden** the house.

6 The woman is **spiteoop** the shop.

7 The house is **rane** the car.

8 The shop is in **tornf** of the man.

B Look at sentences 1–8 in Exercise 5A and the picture below. Find and correct four sentences.

⑤ GIVING DIRECTIONS

6 Complete the conversation with the words in the box.

> ~~are~~   next   the   no   of   near
> there   left

                        are
A: Excuse me, where the cakes?

B: Do you see the fruit over?

A: Where?

B: Over there, the magazines.

A: Yes, I see it.

B: Well, the cakes are to the fruit. On the left.

A: Let me check that. They're on the left the fruit.

B: Right.

A: On right?

B: No, you were right. On the.

A: I see. Thank you.

B: problem.

READING AND GRAMMAR

1 A Read the article. What happened to Jim Black?

BUSINESSMAN, 35, DIES IN HOTEL

This morning, Rose Green, a cleaner at the Adolfi Hotel, Edinburgh, found millionaire businessman Jim Black dead behind the hotel. Police think he died between 10 o'clock and midnight last night. Mr Black and his wife, Carla, were at the hotel with Black's business partner, Mike Brown.

B Work in pairs and complete the police's questions to Mike Brown.

1 be / you / Jim / friends?
Were you and Jim friends?
2 you / see / Jim / yesterday afternoon?
3 you / have / dinner / Jim and Carla?
4 What time / you / go / your room?
5 Where / be / you / between ten o'clock and midnight?

C Read Mike's police statement and answer questions 1–5 above.

WITNESS STATEMENT

Jim Black was a good friend and we were business partners. We sometimes visited places together at weekends – me, Jim and his wife Carla. Carla didn't like me, and she wasn't happy with Jim. I think Carla killed Jim.

Yesterday afternoon I played tennis with Jim for an hour. We started at two o'clock and then at half past three, we went to our rooms in the hotel. I met Jim and Carla at seven o'clock in the restaurant. Jim was very quiet, but Carla talked a lot. I think Jim was angry with her, but I don't know why. We ate dinner together and after that I went to my room at ten. I think Jim went out. I didn't go to bed. I wasn't tired and so I listened to the radio. I went to bed at half past eleven.

Mike Brown

2 A Complete Carla's police statement with the past form of the verbs in brackets.

WITNESS STATEMENT

Jim [1] *was* (be) my husband. Jim and Mike [2]_____ (be) in business together, but they [3]_____ (not be) friends. Mike [4]_____ (not like) Jim.

Yesterday afternoon they [5]_____ (play) tennis. I [6]_____ (walk) to the shops and then I [7]_____ (go) back to the hotel at half past four and [8]_____ (write) some letters. Jim [9]_____ (come) back at six. He [10]_____ (not talk) to me. He was very angry. We [11]_____ (meet) Mike for dinner at seven. Jim was very quiet, so I talked a lot. We [12]_____ (have) dinner, then Mike went to his room at ten. Jim and I danced from ten to eleven, and then Jim [13]_____ (want) to take a walk. He went out and I went to our room. I [14]_____ (be) very tired, so I went to bed. The next morning Jim was dead. I think Mike killed my husband.

Carla Black

B Underline two differences between Carla's and Mike's statements.

C Work in pairs and check your answers.

LISTENING AND GRAMMAR

3 A ▶ C4.1   Listen to five people at the Adolfi Hotel and complete the times in the table.

Name	Information	Time
1 Receptionist	a) Mr Black and Mr Brown went out.	1.45
	b) They went back to their hotel rooms.	_____
2 Waiter	Two men and a woman left the restaurant.	_____
3 Hotel guest	The radio was on in the Blacks' room.	_____
4 Night receptionist	a) Mr Black went out.	_____
	b) Another man went out.	_____
5 Hotel guest	I came back to the hotel.	_____

B Listen again. Are the sentences true (T) or false (F)?

1 Mr Black came back to the hotel alone. *F*

2 A man and a woman danced for half an hour in the restaurant.

3 Two people went out of the hotel at 10.15p.m.

4 The other person was Mr Brown.

5 The other person was a woman.

C Work in pairs. Who do you think killed Jim Black?

SPEAKING

4 A Work in groups. Students A and B: turn to page 149. Other students in the group: you are police officers. Read the information and put the words in 1–4 in the correct order to make questions.

> On Monday at half past one in the afternoon there was a robbery at a clothes shop. Police think it was two students from your class. The students say they were at a restaurant.

1 restaurant / arrive / What / at / you / the / did / time?

2 name / was / the / restaurant's / What?

3 you / did / eat / What?

4 cost / much / it / How / did?

B Work in pairs and write two more questions for Students A and B.

C Half the police officers: ask all the questions to Student A. The other half of the police officers: ask all the questions to Student B. Then change.

D Work in pairs and compare Student A's and Student B's answers. How many answers are different?

SOUNDS: /ʌ/ AND /ʊ/

5 A ▶ C4.2   Listen to the sounds. Then listen again and repeat.

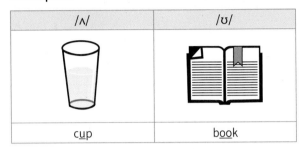

/ʌ/	/ʊ/
c<u>u</u>p	b<u>oo</u>k

B ▶ C4.3   Listen and put the words in the box in the correct group. Then listen again and repeat.

~~lunch~~   ~~put~~   good   m<u>o</u>nth   c<u>ou</u>ntry   cook
h<u>u</u>ngry   l<u>oo</u>k   c<u>o</u>lour   f<u>u</u>ll

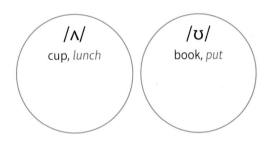

/ʌ/
cup, *lunch*

/ʊ/
book, *put*

6 A Work in pairs. Complete the words and circle the sound in each word.

	/ʌ/
four family words	m(o)ther _____
	b_____
	h_____
	s_____
a type of transport in a city	b_____
a big country	R_____
two days of the week	S_____
	M_____
a number	o_____

	/ʊ/
a sport	f_____
you read it and like it	a g_____
	b_____
two signs on a door	p_____
	p_____
a month	J_____
a food	s_____

B Work with another pair and compare.

9 shopping

ASTE OF MONEY p96 | THE RIGHT GIFT p98 | I'D LIKE A … p100 | THE BORROWING SHOP p102

SPEAKING **9.1** Talk about how you spend money **9.2** Find the right gift **9.3** Ask people to do things **9.4** Describe a favourite possession

LISTENING **9.1** Listen to a radio programme about shopping mistakes **9.3** Listen to someone shopping **9.4** Watch a BBC programme about a borrowing shop

READING **9.2** Read an infographic about gift-giving around the world

WRITING **9.1** Write listings **9.4** Write about a favourite / very useful possession

BBC
INTERVIEWS

Do you like shopping?

G object pronouns
P connected speech: linking
V money

VOCABULARY

MONEY

1 A Work in pairs and discuss. Do you like shopping? Why?/Why not? Where do you usually go? How often?

B Work in pairs. Look at the verbs in bold and underline the correct alternatives.

1 You see something you want in a shop. You want it, but you don't need it. Do you …
   a) walk out of the shop?
   b) *buy/sell* it and then never use it?
2 You have a lot of things at home. You don't need everything. Do you …
   a) *buy/sell* things on the internet?
   b) give things to friends?
3 How much did you *pay/cost* for your last coffee or tea? Do you think it was …
   a) too much?
   b) the right price?
4 How much does transport *pay/cost* you every week? Is this …
   a) too much?
   b) OK?
5 It's your birthday. You *get/give* an expensive gift, but you hate it. Do you …
   a) keep it but never use it?
   b) give it to someone else?

C Work in pairs and take turns. Ask and answer questions 1–5.

2 A Write the past forms of the verbs. Check in your dictionary.

1 buy _____
2 sell _____
3 pay _____
4 cost _____
5 give _____
6 get _____

B ▶ 9.1 Listen and repeat the verbs and sentences.

C Work in pairs and take turns. Student A: say a verb. Student B: say the past form.

▷ page 146 **PHOTOBANK**

LISTENING

3 A Match the words in the box with pictures A–E.

| a hat   drums   a lamp   an exercise bike   a tent |

B Look at the pictures and discuss in pairs. Do you have any of the objects? Which are good things to have? Which are a waste of money?

C ▶ 9.2 Listen to people talk about their shopping mistakes. Match speakers 1–5 with pictures A–E.

1 ____ 2 ____ 3 ____ 4 ____ 5 ____

D Work in groups. Look at the shopping mistakes. Choose one mistake and tell the other students about it.

- wrong size
- didn't use it
- didn't like it
- it didn't work
- too small
- too big
- broke it
- wrong colour

A: *I bought a tablet computer. It was good but my brother broke it.*
B: *How did he break it?*
A: *He sat on it.*

GRAMMAR

OBJECT PRONOUNS

4 A Complete the sentences from the listening with the words in the box. Do **not** use one of the words.

> ~~me~~ you them us it her him

1 My wife bought ___*me*___ an exercise bike for my birthday. I used _____ three times.
2 My boyfriend wanted to go camping so I bought _____ a tent.
3 I phoned _____ yesterday, but she didn't answer.
4 He loves those drums. He plays _____ every day.
5 My mother gave _____ a lamp, but we didn't like it.

B Look at sentences 1–5 above and complete the table.

subject pronoun	object pronoun
I	*me*
you	*you*
he	_____
she	_____
it	_____
we	_____
they	_____

C Underline the correct alternatives in the rules.

RULES

1 Use a subject pronoun *before/after* a verb.
2 Use an object pronoun *before/after* a verb.

D ▶ **9.3** CONNECTED SPEECH: linking Listen to the sentences. Notice how we link the verbs and the object pronouns. Then listen and repeat.

I used‿it.   I bought‿him a tent.
She gave‿us a lamp.   I phoned‿her yesterday.

▷ page 134 **LANGUAGEBANK**

5 A Complete the sentences with an object pronoun.

1 My bag? I bought ___*it*___ in Spain.
2 My shoes? I got _____ from a shop near here.
3 My mobile? I don't often use _____.
4 My last birthday? My sister gave _____ a pen.
5 Did you see me last night? I saw _____.
6 Homework in our class? Our teacher gives _____ homework every night.
7 A student called Maria? I don't know _____.
8 A student called Stefan? I know _____.

B Change the sentences so they are true for you.

My bag? I bought it in Portugal.

C Work in pairs and compare your answers.

WRITING

LISTINGS

6 A Read the listings. Which thing do you think costs the most?

New women's boots, size 38. Black leather.
I got the boots in Madrid but the boots are the wrong size.

DVD of Beyoncé Live at Roseland
I saw Beyoncé at the Roseland concert in New York City in 2011. Beyoncé was fantastic – I really like Beyoncé – and the DVD is great too, but I never watch the DVD because I don't have a DVD player.

For sale: Honda 500T
I bought my Honda 500T in 2004. My Honda 500T is a beautiful motorbike but I don't use my Honda 500T much now.

A signed photo of Brad Pitt
I met Brad Pitt in Sydney last year. Brad Pitt gave me two photos and I want to sell one of the photos.

B Rewrite the listings using pronouns.

1 New women's boots, size 38. Black leather.
        them   *They*
   I got ~~the boots~~ in Madrid. ~~The boots~~ are the wrong size.

C Work in pairs. Write listings for two objects to sell online. Use pronouns where possible.

D Work in groups and read your listings. Which object do you think is best?

SPEAKING

7 A Work alone and think of examples of the things below. Make notes.

* something that was a waste of money
electric guitar – never played
* something big you bought last year
* something you really want to buy now
* something you sold because you didn't like it
* something you gave to someone for free

B Work in pairs and compare your answers.

A: *Tell me something that was a waste of money.*
B: *An electric guitar. I bought it but I never played it.*
A: *Why not?*
B: *I didn't have time. OK, tell me something big you bought last year.*

G like, love, hate + -ing
P sentence stress
V activities

Gift giving around the world

**People love gifts but it's easy to give the wrong thing.
What's the right gift in your country?**

In China, even numbers (6, 8, 10 …) are lucky but in both China and Japan, the word 'four' also means 'death', so people don't like getting a gift of four glasses, for example. And money? In India and Tibet, always give money in odd numbers (1,3,5 …).

Flowers are usually great gifts but be careful. In Australia and Germany red roses are for lovers and in Mexico red flowers are unlucky. In Russia, don't give an even number of flowers – that's for funerals!

Fruit is a popular gift in some countries. In China, pears mean a problem in the family. But peaches are a great gift – they mean long life!

In Canada, people usually open gifts immediately. But in other countries, for example Thailand, people wait and open gifts later.

In the US, it's polite to send a thank you note or email. In Zimbabwe, people like saying 'thank you' by dancing or jumping.

In the UK 'activity' gifts are popular but be careful to match the person and the activity. For example, your friend hates flying, so don't give him a parachute jump.

READING

1 Work in pairs and discuss. When do you give gifts? Who do you give gifts to?

2 A Read the text. Which things are the same as your country?

B Work in pairs and cover the text. Which countries are the sentences about?

1 Send a thank you note. *the US*
2 Peaches are good.
3 Don't give four gifts.
4 People often give 'activities'.
5 It isn't OK to open gifts immediately.
6 People don't like getting eight flowers.
7 Red roses are sometimes a bad idea.
8 51, 101 and 501 are good amounts for money gifts.

C Read the text again and check your ideas.

D Complete the sentences. Then work in pairs and tell your partner.

1 In my country, good gifts are …
2 On my last birthday, I got …
3 On my friend's last birthday, I gave him/her …

GRAMMAR

LIKE, LOVE, HATE + -ING

3 A Look at the sentences. Put the verbs in bold on the line.
People **love** gifts.
People **don't like** getting a gift of four glasses.
People **like** saying 'thank you' by dancing or jumping.
Your friend **hates** flying …

¹love	²	³	⁴
✓✓	✓	✗	✗✗

B Look at the table below and underline the correct alternative in rules 1 and 2.

I/We	love like	flowers. going shopping.
He/She	doesn't like hates	flying. chocolates.
Do you Does he	like	peaches? getting gifts?

RULES
1 Use *love, (not) like, hate* + singular/plural noun.
2 Use *love, (not) like, hate* + verb/verb + *-ing*

▷ page 134 **LANGUAGEBANK**

C ▶ **9.4** SENTENCE STRESS Listen to the sentences and underline the stressed words. Then listen again and repeat.

4

A Complete the sentences with the *-ing* form of the verbs in the box. Pay attention to the spelling.

~~eat~~ live get up go read watch wrap have

1 I love _____eating_____ vegetables.
2 I hate _____ sport on TV.
3 I like _____ two sisters.
4 I don't like _____ in bed.
5 I like _____ to parties.
6 I love _____ in a city.
7 I don't like _____ before eight o'clock.
8 I hate _____ gifts.

B Tick the sentences that are true for you. Change the ones that are false.

I hate eating vegetables.

C Work in pairs and find two things the same for you and your partner.

A: *I hate eating vegetables.*
B: *I like vegetables. I love eating ice cream.*
A: *Me too.*

VOCABULARY

ACTIVITIES

5

A Write the *-ing* form of the verbs to make activities.

1 run*ning*
2 relax_____
3 cook _____
4 swim_____
5 camp _____
6 play_____ computer games
7 take_____ photos
8 go_____ to the theatre
9 chat_____ online
10 go_____ for long walks

B Which activities above do you usually do:

• outside?   • in special clothes?
• inside?   • with a machine?
• with someone?

C Work in pairs and take turns. Ask and answer about the activities. Start with *Do you like … ?*

A: *Do you like running?*
B: *No, I hate it. I never run. What about you? Do you like running?*
A: *Yes, a lot. I run every day.*

speakout TIP

Short answers give a lot of information. Look at the different ways to answer the question, *Do you like … ?*
No, not at all. No, not really. It's/They're OK. It depends. Yes, sometimes. Yes, I do. Yes, a lot.
Write them in your phrasebook.

▷ page 147 **PHOTOBANK**

SPEAKING

6

A Look at the website. Which activities are in the photos?

ACTIVITYGIFTS

Give your friends and family a very special gift. Here are our top ten suggestions:

• hot-air balloon trip
• theatre evening
• driving a Formula-1 car
• salsa lessons
• sushi-making class
• chocolate-making class
• bird-watching tour
• dinner for two
• one-to-one tennis class
• day at a beauty spa

B Work in pairs and take turns. Ask questions to complete the information.

	love	like	not like	hate
taking photos		✓		
being outside				
cooking				
sweets				
relaxing				
dancing				
eating out				
watching plays				
driving fast				
doing exercise				

A: *Do you like taking photos?*
B: *Yes, I do.*
A: *Do you like being outside?*
B: *Yes, a lot.*
A: *How about a hot-air balloon trip?*

C Work alone and choose the best activity gift from the website for your partner. Then tell your partner the gift.

D Tell the class about your activity gift. Was it right for you? Why?/Why not?

F making requests
P word stress; intonation
V shopping departments

VOCABULARY

SHOPPING DEPARTMENTS

1 A Work in pairs and look at pictures A–F. Where do you buy these things in your town/city?

B Look at the store guide and match the departments with pictures A–F.

Furniture & Lighting Bed & Bath Travel & Luggage Sky Restaurant	**3**
Children's clothes & Shoes Toys Computers & Phones Home entertainment Sports	**2**
Women's clothes & Shoes Star café	**1**
Beauty Jewellery & Watches Menswear & Shoes	**G**

C ▶ 9.5 WORD STRESS Listen to the department names and underline the stressed syllable. Then listen again and repeat.

2 A Work in pairs. Choose five departments and list two other things you find in each one.

B Work with a new partner and take turns. Student A: you are a customer. Ask about one of the things on your list. Student B: you are a shop assistant. Answer Student A.

A: Excuse me. I want to buy a laptop. Which department is it?
B: That's Computers and Phones on the second floor.
A: Thank you.

FUNCTION

MAKING REQUESTS

3 A ▶ 9.6 Listen to the conversations and tick the correct answers.

1 Tom wants a World Cup
  a) football shirt. **b)** DVD.
2 Lisa goes first to
  a) the Sports Department. **b)** Home Entertainment.
3 Lisa
  a) finds a gift for Tom. **b)** doesn't find a gift.

B ▶ 9.7 Complete the sentences. Then listen and check.

1 I'd _____ a DVD.
2 Can you _____ me a DVD of the World Cup?
3 _____ you help me?
4 Yes, I _____ like a football DVD.
5 Can _____ see it?
6 Can I _____ this one, please?

C Look at the table and underline the correct alternative in the rules.

I'd	like	a computer game, please.
Can I	see	that one, please?
Can you	help	me, please?

RULES	**1** *I'd like = I like/Can I have* **2** *Can I = Please do something for me/I want to do something* **3** *Can you = Please do something for me/I want to do something*

▷ page 134 **LANGUAGEBANK**

4 A Put the words in the correct order to make conversations.

1 **A:** you? / I / help / Can
  B: like / those / please / I'd / of / one / cakes, / Yes,

2 **A:** photo / Can / a / us, / take / of / please? / you
  B: over / stand / there? / you / can / Sure,

3 **A:** these / two / of / have / we / Can / please? / T-shirts
  B: like? / you / would / colours / which / Yes,

4 **A:** a / like / I'd / please / cappuccino.
  B: you / chocolate / it / Would / like / on?

B ▷ 9.8 **INTONATION** Listen to the intonation and circle the correct letter: P (polite) or NP (not polite).

1 Can you help me?
  a) P NP **b)** P NP

2 Can I have this one?
  a) P NP **b)** P NP

3 Would you like a coffee?
  a) P NP **b)** P NP

4 I'd like a tea, please.
  a) P NP **b)** P NP

C ▷ 9.9 Listen again and repeat the polite sentences.

D Work in pairs and take turns. Student A: read out a request from Exercise 4B. Student B: listen and say *polite* or *not polite*.

LEARN TO

USE HESITATION PHRASES

5 A Look at the sentences from the conversation in Exercise 3A. Underline six different ways to give yourself time to think.

A: What do you want for your birthday?
B: <u>Oh, I don't know</u>. Let me think … . Um … well … maybe something from the World Cup.

A: Which DVD is best?
B: Er … let me see … this one has all the important matches.

speakout TIP

When you need time to think, use hesitation phrases: *Er/Um …*, *Let me think/see/look …*, *Well … .*
What sounds or words do you use in your language to do this?

B ▷ 9.10 Listen to the questions and use hesitation phrases before you answer.

C Work in pairs. Student A: turn to page 149. Student B: turn to page 153. Ask and answer the questions. Use hesitation phrases.

SPEAKING

6 A Work in pairs and complete the conversation.

Student A	Student B
What / you / like / your birthday?	(hesitate) I / like / **new pen**.
What colour / you / like?	(hesitate) Can / get /me / **a black one?**

B Work in pairs and take turns. Practise the conversation.

C Work alone. Write three things you would like for your birthday.

D Work in pairs and practise the conversation with different gifts. Change the words in bold.

DVD PREVIEW

1 Work in pairs and discuss. Do you ever borrow things? Who do you borrow from? What do you borrow?

2 A Which items in the box are in the photos below?

> a book   ice skates   a toy   a coffee maker   a DVD
> a mixer   a baby carrier   a bike helmet   a dress
> a bike   a power tool   a jacket

B Which items in the box in Exercise 2A are OK to borrow, and which only to buy? Write two lists. Then compare with your partner.

OK to borrow:

Only buy:

C Read the programme information and answer the questions.

1 What items are <u>not</u> in the box in Exercise 2A?
2 What is the name of the shop? Where is it?
3 How is the shop different?
4 How many members does the shop have?

◀)) Leila, the 'borrowing shop'

BBC

Do you need a suitcase for your holiday and you don't want to buy one? Plates and cups for a party? Toys for your child? Then go to your local 'borrowing shop' and get them. In this programme we visit Leila, the original borrowing shop in Berlin, where over 400 local people go to borrow things they need.

DVD VIEW

3 A Write three items from your list of 'OK to borrow' from Exercise 2B in your notebook. Watch the DVD. Does the shop have your three items?

B Is the information below true (T) or false (F)? Correct the false information in each sentence. Watch the DVD again and check.

1 Customers buy things from the shop.
2 To become a member, you bring one item to the shop.
3 When a member borrows something, the shop puts their name in the computer.
4 You borrow things for a short or long time.
5 The people in the shop want to start borrowing things in other cities.

C Work in pairs and choose the correct alternatives. Then watch the DVD again to check your answers.

1 I've got a car coffee machine, baby carrier, ice skates, plates and cups, power tools … *Stuff/Things* like this.
2 So each member has to bring an item *they have/of their own* to the shop and that's their membership *money/fee*.
3 Today I would like to have a helmet for my child because I'm getting a children's *seat/carrier* for the bike.
4 It's a great idea because I have so many things at home that I don't need, and I would love to bring them and get something that I need *in return/back*.
5 I probably make a cake once a year, it's coming and just getting a mixer for the day. It's *genius/a great idea*. I would love to see this in places like Chicago.

D Work with other students and discuss. Is the borrowing shop a good idea for your city or town? Why?/Why not?

speakout a favourite possession

4 A Think about one of your favourite or most useful possessions. Use the questions below to make notes about it.

Possession: _____
- Where did you get it?
- Where is it now?
- What do you do with it?
- Why do you like it?

Other information: _____

B Work in pairs and take turns. Ask and answer the questions above.

C ▶ 9.11 Listen to someone talk about a favourite or very useful possession and answer the questions in Exercise 4A.

D Listen again and tick the key phrases you hear.

KEY PHRASES

One of my favourite [things/possessions] is …
My most useful [thing/possession] is …
It's [very small/big/red/…].
I keep it [in my bag/pocket/at home].
I bought it [last year/in New York/…].
[My brother/wife/best friend/…] gave it to me …
for [my birthday/Christmas/…]
I like it because it's [easy to use/useful/beautiful].
I use it [all the time/a lot].

5 A Work with a new partner. Practise talking about your possession. Use the key phrases to help.

B Work in groups and take turns. Tell other students about your possession.

writeback a useful possession

6 A Read the text. Which questions from Exercise 4A does it answer?

My bike

My most useful possession is my bike. My friends gave it to me for my eighteenth birthday. It's a 1990s TREK 720. It's now twenty years old but I like it because it's good in all types of weather. It's also good in the city. I ride it to work every day and I keep it in the street near my workplace. At home I keep it in the garden. It's not new, but it's a fantastic little bike.

B Write a description of a favourite or very useful possession. Write 80–100 words.

ⓥ MONEY

1 A Put the letters in the correct order to make verbs.

1 ybu *buy*   4 tocs
2 vegi   5 etg
3 lels   6 apy

B Complete the sentences with the correct form of the verbs above.

1 I ___*buy*___ a new mobile phone once a year.
2 Food _____ too much in my country.
3 My manager _____ me well and I have long holidays.
4 I _____ money to poor people.
5 For my birthday I always _____ clothes from my family.
6 I never _____ things to my friends. I don't want their money.

C Tick the sentences in Exercise 1B that you agree with. Then compare with a partner.

ⓖ OBJECT PRONOUNS

2 A Match sentences 1–6 with a)–f). Use the underlined pronoun to help.

1 I don't know <u>them</u>. *f*
2 I hate <u>it</u>.
3 <u>They</u> cook us food.
4 I like <u>him</u>.
5 <u>They</u> often phone me.
6 I saw <u>her</u> yesterday.

a) my sister
b) my friends
c) chefs
d) ice cream
e) Ben Affleck
f) The Rolling Stones

B Write people and things that are true for you for 1–6.

1 I don't know them.
The students in the next class.

C Work in pairs and take turns. Student A: say one thing on your list. Student B: say the sentence that matches.

A: The students in the next class.
B: You don't know them.
A: Yes!
B: I know two of them.

ⓖ LIKE, LOVE, HATE + -ING

3 A Complete the questions.

1 you / like / read?
Do you like reading?
2 What / you / like / read?
3 What / TV programme / you / like / watch?
4 Who / you / like / phone?
5 What / you / like / eat / for dinner?
6 you / like / fly?
7 What / sport / like / do?
8 What / music / like / listen / to?

B Work in pairs and take turns. Ask and answer the questions. Say one thing you like or love, and one thing you hate.

I love reading newspapers, but I hate reading the news online.

ⓥ ACTIVITIES

4 A Add the vowels to complete the activities.

1 c_mp_ng
2 c_ _k_ng
3 g_ _ng f_r l_ng w_lks
4 ch_tt_ng _nl_n_
5 r_nn_ng
6 g_ _ng t_ th_ th_ _tr_
7 pl_y_ng c_mp_t_r g_m_s
8 r_l_x_ng
9 t_k_ng ph_t_s
10 sw_mm_ng

B Work in pairs and take turns. Student A: choose an activity. Think of the place you do it and an object you need. Student B: ask questions and guess the activity.

B: Where do you do it?
A: In the countryside.
B: What do you need?
A: A tent.
B: Camping?
A: Yes!

ⓥ SHOPPING DEPARTMENTS

5 A Correct the spelling mistakes in each department name.

1 Jewellery & Waches
2 Computers & Fones
3 Furniture & Liting
4 Travel & Lugage
5 Home Entertanement
6 Bed & Batth
7 Menswhere & Shoes
8 Beautey
9 Childrins clothes & Shoes
10 Toyz

B Work in pairs and discuss. What's your favourite department in a store or on an online store? What do you usually buy there?

ⓕ MAKING REQUESTS

6 A Find and correct seven mistakes in the conversation.

A: I̶ ̶c̶a̶n̶ help you? *Can I*
B: Yes, I would this **pen**.
A: OK. Is he a present?
B: Er … yes. Can I wrap it for me?
A: Of course. Which wrapping paper you would like – **red** or **green**?
B: I'd like the **green** paper.
A: Where is the gift for?
B: For I. Today is my birthday!

B Work in pairs and practise the conversation.

C Work alone. Change the words in bold for your part (A or B).

D Work in pairs. Practise the new conversation.

10 plans

A NEW JOB p106   TIME FOR A CHANGE p108   HELLO AND GOODBYE p110   MIRANDA p112

SPEAKING 10.1 Discuss the best job for you 10.2 Talk about plans 10.3 Start and end conversations 10.4 Talk about when you tried something new

LISTENING 10.2 Listen to job interviews 10.2 Listen to street interviews about people's goals 10.3 listen to people start and end conversations 10.4 Watch a BBC programme about someone who wants to change their life

READING 10.1 Read about jobs

WRITING 10.2 Check your writing 10.4 Write an interview

BBC
INTERVIEWS

◗◗) What did you want to be?

G **G** can/can't

P **P** strong and weak forms: can/can't

V **V** collocations

VOCABULARY

COLLOCATIONS

1 A Work in pairs and complete the word webs with the verbs in the box.

~~cook~~ ride speak use play make read remember

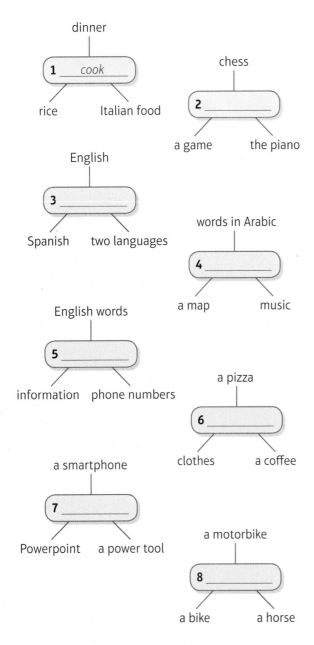

1 dinner / **cook** / rice / Italian food

2 chess / a game / the piano

3 English / Spanish / two languages

4 words in Arabic / a map / music

5 English words / information / phone numbers

6 a pizza / clothes / a coffee

7 a smartphone / Powerpoint / a power tool

8 a motorbike / a bike / a horse

B Work in pairs. Student A: say a verb. Student B: say three nouns that go with the verb. Student A: add more nouns.

A: *read*
B: *read music, read a map, read Arabic*
A: *read a book, read a newspaper*

jobs

1 Tour guide

Tourist service needs a tour guide to take small groups of tourists on visits to the old town. You need to speak English and one other language, and you need a good memory for facts. Driving licence also needed. Contact us.

2 Office manager

We are a large city office and sell computers to international businesses. We need an office manager for our sales department. You need to be very organised, good with people and have good telephone skills. You also need to manage our website and use Word, Excel and Powerpoint. Apply online.

3 Pizza delivery person

Can you ride a motorbike? Do you know the city well? Are you friendly but can you also work alone? We are a small pizza business. We need a delivery person to take pizzas to people's houses. Sometimes we need help in the kitchen, cleaning and cooking. Contact us for more details.

4 Airport shop assistant

A chance to join a busy team in our duty-free shop at Terminal 5. We sell watches, cameras, laptops, perfume, make-up, sunglasses and other high-class items. Are you friendly, polite and good with people? Can you work fast in a busy international shop? Hours: 5a.m.–2p.m. or 2p.m.–10.00p.m. Apply online.

READING

2 A Read the job adverts above. Which job is best for you? Which one isn't good for you? Why?

B Read about jobs 1–4 again. Correct the sentences below. Two sentences are correct.

1 **a)** You need to speak three languages.
   b) You need a car.
2 **a)** You sell computers to local businesses.
   b) You work with people a lot.
3 **a)** You need to live in the city.
   b) You work in the kitchen every day.
4 **a)** You work alone in the shop.
   b) You have the morning or afternoon free.

3 A ▶ 10.1 Listen to three interviews. Which jobs from the adverts do the people want? Do they get the jobs?

B Listen again. What's one good point and one bad point about each person?

GRAMMAR

CAN/CAN'T

4 A Complete the sentences with *can* or *can't*.

	you	ride a motorbike?
_____		make pizzas?
Yes,	I	_____.
No,		_____.

+	I/You/He/	_____	speak
	She		English.
–	We/They	_____	drive.

B Underline the correct alternative to complete the rule.

> **RULES**
>
> Use *can* or *can't* to talk about *your ability/ activities you do every day.*

C ▶ 10.2 **STRONG AND WEAK FORMS:** *can/can't*
Listen. Then listen again and repeat.

1 I can cook.   /kən/
2 Can you cook?   /kən/
3 Yes, I can.   /kæn/
4 No, I can't.   /kɑːnt/

D ▶ 10.3 Listen to six sentences. Which of the sounds (a, b or c) do you hear? Write the number.

a) /kən/ *1*   b) /kæn/   c) /kɑːnt/

▷ page 136 **LANGUAGEBANK**

5 A Correct the mistakes in five of the questions.

1 Can you to play tennis? *Can you play tennis?*
2 Cans she use a power tool?
3 Does Barbara can ride a horse?
4 Can dance you?
5 Can you and your friend speak Italian?
6 Can George reads Chinese?

B Write answers to the questions above.

1 No, I ___*can't*___, but I ___*can*___ play football.
2 Yes, _____ _____.
3 No, _____ _____.
4 Yes, _____ _____, and _____ _____ sing, too.
5 No, _____ _____, but _____ _____ _____ Spanish.
6 Yes, _____ _____, but _____ _____ speak Chinese.

▷ page 147 **PHOTOBANK**

SPEAKING

6 A Work in pairs and do the questionnaire. Write 1–5 for each activity.

5 = Yes, very well.
4 = Yes, I can.
3 = Yes, quite well.
1 = Yes, but not vey well.
0 = No, I can't.

B Take turns to ask questions and complete the questionnaire for your partner.

A: *Can you dance?*
B: *Yes, I can, but not very well.*

What is your perfect job?
Look at the skills below. What can you do?

A		B		C	
dance	☐	play football	☐	play chess	☐
sing	☐	play tennis	☐	read a map	☐
act	☐	ride a horse	☐	speak another language	☐
play the guitar or the piano	☐	run five kilometres	☐	remember information	☐

C Turn to the key on page 151. What's the best job for your partner?

D Work in pairs and answer the questions.

1 Do you think the questionnaire is right about you?
2 What job would you like?

A: *The questionnaire says a good job for me is in sports, but I'd like to be a doctor. I like helping people. What about you?*
B: *I'd like to be a …*

G be going to
P weak form: *going to*
V life changes

Top ten goals

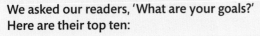

People often want to make changes in their life: their job, their lifestyle, their relationships. They talk about it, they buy a self-help book ... but usually nothing changes, and then a year later the same goal comes back again. They say, 'This time, I'm really going to make a change!'

We asked our readers, 'What are your goals?' Here are their top ten:

1 stop smoking
2 get fit
3 spend more time with friends and family
4 work less and relax more
5 help others
6 get organised
7 lose weight
8 learn something new
9 save money
10 change jobs

VOCABULARY

LIFE CHANGES

1 A Work in pairs and write four things people often want to change in their lives.

People often want to …

B Read the list of top ten goals above. Which ones can you see in the pictures?

C Read the list again. Work in pairs. Do you want to do any of these things?

A: I want to get organised.
B: Me too! And I want to …

LISTENING

2 A ▶ 10.4 Listen to five people talk about their goals. Write the number(s) from the list in Exercise 1A next to the name.

1 Tom _____8_____   3 Liam _____   5 Alex _____
2 Fiona _____   4 Rudi _____

B Listen again. Are the sentences true (T) or false (F)?

1 Tom's girlfriend can't cook.
2 He wants to learn Japanese cooking.
3 Fiona wants to work in an office.
4 Liam plans to stop watching TV.
5 Rudi's a good tennis player.
6 He plans to walk a lot.
7 Alex plans to spend more time with her friends.
8 She likes shopping.

C Work in pairs and discuss. Which people are similar to you? Why?

GRAMMAR

BE GOING TO

3 A Look at sentences a)–d) and answer the questions.

1 Are they about the present or future?
2 Which are positive (+) and negative (–)?

a) I'm going to learn to cook.
b) My friend Sheila is going to help me.
c) Then you aren't going to save money!
d) Yes, but I'm not going to stop shopping.

B Complete the table.

+	I'_m_	going	change jobs.
	You'___		work less.
	She'___		get fit.
–	He ___		be there.
	We ___		come.

C Put the words in the correct order to make questions.

1 are / do / you / to / What / going / ?
2 she / work / Where / going / is / to / ?

D ▷ **10.5** WEAK FORM: *going to*
Listen and check your answers to Exercises 3B and 3C. Then listen again and repeat. Pay attention to the pronunciation of *going to* /ɡəʊɪŋtə/.

▷ page 136 **LANGUAGEBANK**

4 A Add words to make sentences with *be going to*.

1 After class, / I / have / a coffee.
After class, I'm going to have a coffee.
2 I / not / do / the homework / tonight.
3 I / not / write / any emails / tomorrow.
4 Tomorrow afternoon, / I / relax.
5 On Friday, / my friends and I / see a film.

B Tick the plans above that are true for you. Change the ones that are not true.

C Work in pairs and compare your answers.

A: What are you going to do after class?
B: I'm going to have a coffee. What about you?
A: I'm not going to have a coffee. I'm going to have lunch.

D Work in groups. Say one thing about your partner's plans and one thing about your plans.

Tomorrow afternoon, Jan's going to relax, but I'm going to play football in the park.

SPEAKING

5 A Look at the picture. Write your five plans or goals in the boxes. Use the pictures on page 108 for ideas.

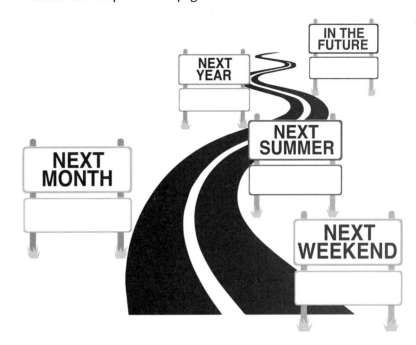

B Work in groups and take turns. Tell other students your plans.

Next summer, I'm going to work in a hotel.

WRITING

CHECKING YOUR WORK

6 A Read the email. Find and correct:

• five mistakes with the punctuation/capitalisation.
• five mistakes with the verbs.

> Hi
> ~~hi~~/Elif, Thanks for your email. Heres the information about my plans for next weekend. I'm going be in Istanbul for three days. Can we to meet? My hotel is the FiveStar in Topsu Street. I going to visit the Blue Mosque on sunday and Id like to look around the markets. Can we have lunch together one day. Are Saturday good for you? Email me or texted me.
>
> Jayne

speakout TIP

After you write something, check your writing. You can check punctuation and verbs. What other things can you check?

B Write an email to another student. Choose one of your plans from Exercise 5 or another plan and arrange a time to meet. Use the email above to help.

C Work in pairs. Check each other's emails. Use your ideas from the Speakout Tip to help.

D Answer your partner's email.

F starting and ending conversations
P sentence stress
V saying goodbye

FUNCTION

STARTING AND ENDING CONVERSATIONS

1 A Work in pairs and answer the questions.

1 How do you say hello and goodbye in your country?

2 When do you start conversations with strangers? What do you say?

At a train station. I ask about the train times or the platform number.

B ▶ 10.6 Listen to the conversations and write friends (F) or strangers (S).

1 _____

2 _____

3 _____

C Listen again. Why does the person end the conversation? Tick the correct reason a)–c).

Conversation 1
a) He wants a coffee.
b) He has a lesson.
c) He has no money for lunch.

Conversation 2
a) She's going to get off the train.
b) She lost her bank card.
c) She doesn't like the man.

Conversation 3
a) She wants to leave the party.
b) She doesn't speak any languages.
c) She thinks he's boring.

2 A Complete the conversations with the words in the box. Then check audio script 10.6 on page 160.

great meet have talk around think friend time

1 A: Hey, this is a ¹ *great* place.
   B: Yes, it's really good. I often come here.

2 B: … Let's have coffee.
   A: OK … wait, is that the ² _____?

3 A: Excuse me, do you ³ _____ the time?
   B: Yes, it's half past four.

4 A: I hope we ⁴ _____ again.

5 A: What do you ⁵ _____ of the music?
   B: It's not bad.

6 A: So are you from ⁶ _____ here?

7 B: I'm sorry, I can see an old ⁷ _____ over there. Nice to ⁸ _____ to you.
   A: Oh … and you.

B Work in pairs and look at the conversations above. Find:

1 four phrases for starting a conversation.
This is a great place.

2 four phrases for finishing a conversation.
Is that the time?

C ▶ 10.7 SENTENCE STRESS Listen and underline the stressed words. Then listen and repeat.

1 What do you think of the music?
2 Are you from around here?
3 Is that the time?
4 Nice to talk to you.

▷ page 136 **LANGUAGEBANK**

3 A Add words to make two conversations.

Conversation 1

Student A

This / be / good / party.

Student B

Yes, / it/ be. What / you / think / food?

It / be / good.

I / be / (your name).

Hi, / I / be / (your name).

You / around / here?

Yes, / I / live in / (place).

Conversation 2

Student A

Student B

be / that / time?

Yes, / eleven o'clock / I / have / business meeting / tomorrow / eight.

And my train / leave / quarter past eleven.

Nice / talk / you.

Yes, / hope / meet again.

B Work in pairs and take turns to practise the conversations.

LEARN TO

USE TWO-PART EXCHANGES

4 A Work in pairs. How can B respond naturally to A?

1 **A:** This is a great place.
   B: _____
2 **A:** Nice to talk to you.
   B: _____
3 **A:** I hope we meet again.
   B: _____
4 **A:** Here's my card.
   B: _____

B ▶ 10.8 Listen and complete the conversations above.

speakout TIP

Two-part exchanges often have alternatives. For example:
A: *How are you?*
B: *Fine, thanks. And you?/Not bad. And you?*

When you write two-part exchanges in your phrasebook, write down at least one alternative response. Write one alternative response for the four sentences in Exercise 4A.

C Work in pairs and take turns. Use the prompts below to practise the two-line conversations in Exercise 4A.

my card   meet again   great place   nice to meet

VOCABULARY

SAYING GOODBYE

5 A Complete the phrases for saying goodbye and leaving. Use audio script 10.6 on page 160 to help.

1 see you s_ _ _ _
2 see you i_ two w_ _ _ _ _
3 keep in t_ _ _ _ _
4 b_ _ _
5 see you l_ _ _ _ _

B Work with other students. Student A: say goodbye. Student B: answer with a different phrase. Then speak to other students.

A: Bye.
B: See you later.

SPEAKING

6 A You are going to role-play a party. Work in pairs and write three ways to start a conversation. You can say/ask something about:

- the food
- the music
- the party
- the other person's plans for the weekend
- last weekend

B Role-play the party. Have conversations with other people. After about one minute, finish the conversation politely and move to another person.

Hi, Luca. This is a great ...

Hi, Jan. What do you think of the ...?

Hi, Marta. What are your plans for ...?

Nice to chat to you.

Is that the time?

DVD PREVIEW

1 A Work in pairs and discuss the questions. Use the ideas below to help. What problems can you have when you:

- learn something new?
- start a new job?
- go to a new place?
- spend time with friends?
- try to get fit?

> You have the wrong clothes.
>
> You break something.　　You feel stupid.
>
> You're bored.　　It's too expensive.
>
> You don't understand what to do.
>
> You don't know the people.　　You make mistakes.
>
> The teacher doesn't like you.
>
> You aren't good at it.

B Read the programme information and answer the questions.

1 What does Miranda want to do?

2 Which things from Exercise 1A does she try?

◁)) Miranda

BBC

Miranda is a BBC comedy show, and Miranda is the star of the show. She's thirty-something, doesn't like her job, doesn't have a boyfriend and wants to meet new people. In this episode Miranda wants to change her life and become the 'New Me.' So she goes to a French class, she starts a new job, she joins a diet club and she goes to a Japanese restaurant with her friends … but for Miranda, there's always a problem!

DVD VIEW

2 A Watch the DVD. Match the problems and the places.

1 the French class

2 the office

3 the diet club

4 the restaurant

a) She gets stuck.

b) Everyone wants to eat pies and sweets.

c) Her trousers get stuck.

d) She knows the teacher.

e) She breaks things.

f) The teacher isn't happy with the group.

B Which phrases did Miranda say? Write M next to them.

a) What is this? M	**f)** Gather please.
b) He's lovely!	**g)** Help yourself.
c) I'm stuck in the chair!	**h)** Thank you very much.
d) I can do this.	**i)** Sorry about this.
e) Good morning.	**j)** Hello again.

C Watch the DVD again to check your answers.

D Work in pairs and look at the sentences from the diet club section of the clip. Number them in order. Then watch the diet club section again and check.

b) No try again. _____

d) Help yourself. _____

c) Look, I am just trying to help you help yourself. _____

a) So which section, to the left, or the right, looks the most delicious? *1*

e) No, not to the buffet, sit down!

speakout something new

3 A Think about a time when you tried to learn something new. Look at the questions below and make notes:

1 What did you try to learn? When? Why?
2 Did you do it alone or with a friend?
3 Did you have a teacher? Was he or she good?
4 What happened?

B Work in pairs and take turns. Ask and answer the questions above.

C ▶ 10.9 Listen to a woman talk about learning something new. Answer the questions in Exercise 3A.

D Listen again and tick the key phrases you hear.

KEY PHRASES

I wanted to learn [to play guitar/to cook/…] because …
I went to a class.
I tried to learn it [alone/with a friend/…].
I was/wasn't [very] good at it.
The teacher was [great/good/not very good].
After [four/six/…] months I [played guitar/did it/…] really well.
I still [do it/play] every day.

---

4 A Work with a new partner and tell each other your stories. Use the key phrases to help.

B Work in groups and take turns. Student A: tell your story. Other students: ask one question.

writeback an interview

5 A Read the start of the magazine interview and answer the questions.

1 What did the person try to learn? Why?
2 Do you know how to do this activity?
3 If yes, do you like it? If no, would you like to learn to do it?

Something new

Q: What did you try to learn?
   A: How to use Twitter.
Q: Why did you want to learn it?
   A: Because all my friends use Twitter.
Q: When was this?
   A: Last summer. I can't remember when exactly.
Q: So, how did you learn?
   A: Well, I asked a friend for help.
Q: What happened?
   A: We tried …

B Write a magazine interview about another student's learning story. Write 80–100 words.

ⓥ COLLOCATIONS

1 A The verbs are in the wrong sentences. Put them in the correct sentence.

1 I often ~~speak~~ Italian food. *cook*
2 I read chess every weekend.
3 It's easy to ride maps.
4 I play two languages.
5 I cook all my clothes.
6 I don't remember Powerpoint in my job.
7 I would like to make a horse.
8 It's easy to use phone numbers.

B Add two more words/phrases to each verb.

cook lunch, cook pasta

C Work in pairs. Which sentences in Exercise 1A are true for you?

ⓖ CAN/CAN'T

2 A Use the words to make five questions with *What … can … ?*

What languages can you speak?

languages
computer programs
sports
food
important dates

cook
speak
play
remember
use

B Work in pairs and take turns. Ask and answer the questions.

ⓥ LIFE CHANGES

3 A Underline the correct alternatives.

1 get *organised*/*new*
2 change *smoking*/*jobs*
3 save *money*/*weight*
4 learn *something new*/*others*
5 spend more *jobs*/*time with friends*
6 work *money*/*less* and relax more
7 help *organised*/*others*
8 stop *smoking*/*fit*
9 lose *weight*/*time with friends*
10 get *less and relax more*/*fit*

B Work in pairs and discuss. Which life changes are easy, and which are difficult?

A: I think it's easy to get organised.
B: For me, it's difficult.

ⓖ BE GOING TO

4 A Look at the list. Write the man's plans for the day.

He's going to buy some milk and cheese at the supermarket.

To do:
Supermarket – milk, cheese
Café – Sue and Jenny
Gym
Cash machine – 200 euros
Newsagent's – newspaper
Pharmacy – aspirin

B Write a list of four places you're going to go to next week.

C Work in pairs. Guess what your partner is going to do in each place.

A: What am I going to do in the park?
B: Are you going to walk there?
A: No. Try again.
B: Are you going to play football?
A: Yes.

ⓕ STARTING AND ENDING CONVERSATIONS

5 A Complete the conversation with the words in the box.

~~are~~   minutes   there
nice (x2)   that   you   do

A: Hi!
B: Oh, hi. How ⌄ you?   *are*
A: **Good**, thanks. This is a **café**.
B: Yes, I sometimes come here for **lunch**.
A: Really? What you think of the **food**?
B: Er … it's good. Wait, is the time?
A: No, that clock's wrong. It's **two** o'clock.
B: Oh no, my **train** leaves in five!
A: No problem. There's a train every half hour.
B: Sorry, I can see **an old friend** over.
A: Oh, OK. to talk to you.
B: You too. See soon …

B Work in pairs and practise the conversation.

C Change the words in bold.

D Work with a new partner. Practise the new conversation.

A: Hi!
B: Oh, hi. How are you?
A: Fine, thanks. This is a nice hotel.
B: Yes, I sometimes come here for dinner.

ⓥ SAYING GOODBYE

6 Find and correct the mistakes.

1 See you late.
2 By.
3 See you one week.
4 Keep on touch.
5 See soon.

What can you do in English?

Now is a good time to stop and think about your learning. Look at the questionnaire. What can you do in English?

√ = yes   × = no   ? = yes, but not very well

		You	Your partner
1	I can count to a hundred and say the alphabet.	○	○
2	I can talk about my family.	○	○
3	I can order food and drink in a café.	○	○
4	I can pronounce /bægz/ and /mʌðə/.	○	○
5	I can ask someone about their daily routines.	○	○
6	I can describe my dinner yesterday evening.	○	○
7	I can tell the time.	○	○
8	I can talk about transport in my town.	○	○
9	I can buy a train ticket.	○	○
10	I can use correct punctuation in my writing.	○	○
11	I can answer questions about my last holiday.	○	○
12	I can use intonation to sound interested.	○	○
13	I can give simple directions in a shop.	○	○
14	I can talk about my likes and dislikes.	○	○
15	I can talk about my plans for next year.	○	○

READING AND GRAMMAR

1 A Work alone and complete the questionnaire for you.

B Work in pairs and take turns. Complete the questionnaire for your partner.

A: Can you … ?
B: Yes, I can. How about you?
C: Yes, I can, but not very well. I need more practice.

C Complete the sentences about you with the words in the box.

> reading   listening   speaking
> writing   grammar   vocabulary
> pronunciation   spelling

1 _____ and _____ English are OK for me.
2 I want to improve my _____ and _____ in English.

D Work in pairs and compare your answers.

2 A Read the text from a student's diary. Then replace the underlined words with the pronouns in the box.

> our̶   she   their   we   they   me   my   her   us   them (×2)   him

Julia, ¹<u>we</u> [our] teacher, often corrects my pronunciation and so I asked ²<u>my teacher</u> to help ³<u>I</u>.
In the next lesson, ⁴<u>Julia</u> took the class to the computer room and gave ⁵<u>our class</u> books.
　　The books were in very easy English and ⁶<u>the books</u> were all different. ⁷<u>Our class</u> read ⁸<u>the books</u> and listened to ⁹<u>the books</u> online. Then we listened again and said the words at the same time as the speaker.
　　I think this is a good way to improve my pronunciation and ¹⁰<u>I</u> friend, Juan, said it was good for ¹¹<u>Juan</u> too. Anna and Yasif have problems with ¹²<u>they</u> listening and they said reading and listening together was a great idea.

B Work in pairs and answer the questions.

1 Do you read books or magazines or websites in English? Which ones?
2 Do you read and listen to books at the same time? Why is this useful?
3 Do you sometimes listen and say the words with the speaker? Why is this useful?

LISTENING AND GRAMMAR

3 A ▶ C5.1   Listen to students talk about learning English. Write the number of the speaker next to the problem.

Speaking
Grammar
Vocabulary *1*
Writing
Listening

B Listen again and underline the correct alternatives.

1 I'm going to learn *seven/ten* new words every day.
2 I'm going to look at the BBC news website and *read/write* down new words.
3 In the *lesson/coffee break*, I'm not going to speak in my language.
4 I'm going to listen to my CD and read the audio scripts at the *same time/sometimes*.
5 I'm going to *write/read* a diary every night, in English.
6 I'm going to write about my *life/day*.

C Which three things in Exercise 3B are the best ideas?

SPEAKING

4 A Work alone. Choose two learning goals from column A.

Make notes about your plans in column B. Use ideas from Exercise 3A and your own ideas.

A	B
I want to improve my …	**so I'm going to …**
reading	
writing	
listening	
speaking	
vocabulary	
grammar	
pronunciation	

B Work in groups and take turns. Tell other students about your plans.

5 Work in groups. Play the Speakout Game on page 117.

SOUNDS: /ɑː/ AND /ɜː/

6 A ▶ C5.2   Listen to the sounds and the words. Then listen and repeat.

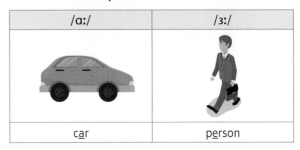

/ɑː/	/ɜː/
car	person

B ▶ C5.3   Listen and put the words in the the correct group. Then listen and repeat.

st~~art~~   w~~ord~~   f~~ir~~st   l~~a~~st   p~~a~~rty   l~~ear~~n   g~~ir~~lfriend   gu~~i~~t~~ar~~ist   c~~a~~n't   w~~or~~k   c~~ir~~cle   d~~a~~nce

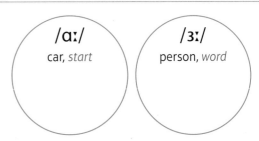

/ɑː/
car, *start*

/ɜː/
person, *word*

7 A Work in pairs. Complete the word and circle the sound in each word.

	/ɑː/
a country	Ⓐrgentina
a yellow fruit	b_____
The 3rd month	M_____
a form of *be*	a_____
not near, but …	f_____
morning, … , evening	a_____
the opposite of soft	l_____

	/ɜː/
Berlin is there	G_____
a colour	p_____
a type of clothes	s_____
a day	Th_____
a form of *be*	w_____
Give me water, I'm …	th_____
a number	th_____

B Work with another pair and compare.

SPEAKOUT GAME

Work in groups and take turns.
Student A: roll the dice and move your counter to the correct square.
Look at the colour of the square and follow the instructions on the square in the same colour at the top.

| Talk for thirty seconds about this | Say and spell three words | Make and ask the question | Say three phrases from this situation |

Start	1 your town/ city or country	2 transport	3 what/you/ usually/do/ at the weekend?	4 ordering in a café	5 your family
11 countries	10 why/you/like/ speak/English?	9 asking for information about a concert	8 a favourite object	7 places	6 what/you/do/ tonight?
12 buying a train ticket	13 shopping	14 drink	15 what/you/do/ last weekend?	16 telling the time	17 your daily routine
23 food	22 you/here/ this time last week?	21 giving directions	20 your diet	19 adjectives for feelings	18 what/your favourite subject/ in school?
24 starting a conversation	25 how you travel	26 colours	27 be/good restaurant/near here?	28 in a hotel	29 your life ten years ago
35 jobs	34 what time/you/ get home/ every day?	33 asking the teacher a classroom question	32 last weekend	31 clothes	30 you/happy?
36 making a request	37 your perfect job	38 office objects	39 when/you/last/ travel/by boat?	40 ending a conversation	Finish!

Is it my turn?

Let's ask the teacher.

It's your turn.

1 LANGUAGE BANK

GRAMMAR

1.1 *be: I/you*

positive			
+	I	'm am	Keira. from Ireland.
	You	're are	

negative			
–	I	'm not am not	Felipa. from Spain.
	You	aren't are not	from here.

I'm = I am. You're = You are. You aren't = You are not. Use contractions (*I'm, you're*) in speaking and informal writing.

questions			
?	Where	am	I?
		are	you	from?
		Am	I	right?
		Are	you	Ed Black? from London?

Use *be* + subject (*I/you*) for questions.

I'm in classroom 3.   **Am I** in classroom 3?

You're Jim.   **Are you** Jim?

short answers		
Yes,	I	am.
	you	are.
No,	I	'm not.
	you	aren't.

Use short answers to *yes/no* questions:
Are you David Snow? Yes, I am ~~David Snow~~.
Don't use contractions in positive short answers: *Yes, I am.* NOT ~~Yes, I'm.~~
Use *be* with names: *I'm Olga.*
Use *be* to say or ask where a person is from: *Are you from Russia?*
Use *be* with ages: *I'm nine.*

1.2 *be: he/she/it*

positive and negative			
+	He She	's is	a doctor. from Germany.
	It		in South Africa.
–	He/She/It	isn't is not	right.

He's, she's, it's = he is, she is, it is.
He isn't, she isn't, it isn't = he is not, she is not, it is not.
Use contractions (*he's, she's,* etc.) in speaking and informal writing.

questions			
?	Where	is	he/she/it	from?
		Is		in Mexico?

short answers		
Yes,	he/she/it	is.
No,		isn't.

Use *be* + subject (*he/she/it*) for questions.

She's a student.   **Is she** a student?

Use short answers to *yes/no* questions: *Is she from Spain? Yes, she is.*
Don't use contractions in positive short answers: *Yes, it is.* NOT ~~Yes, it's.~~
Use *be* + *a/an* to talk about jobs: *I'm a nurse. He's an actor.*

1.3 giving personal information

		first name? surname? nationality? job? phone number? email address?
What's What is	your	

I'm	Argentinian. an engineer.

It's	Marie. 0147385. marie.973@hotmail.com

For email addresses, say: *marie dot nine seven three at hotmail dot com.*
For telephone numbers, for *0*, say *oh* in British English. In American English, say *oh* or *zero*.

PRACTICE

.1 **A** Complete the conversation with words in the box.

'm̶ Am 're I you I'm 'm Are not I'm aren't you're

A: Hi, I ¹ _'m_ Wayne.

B: Hi, ² _____ 'm Fernando.

A: ³ _____ you from Colombia?

B: ⁴ _____ I from Colombia?

A: Yes.

B: No, I'm ⁵ _____.

A: You ⁶ _____ from Colombia. Really?

B: That's right. ⁷ _____ from Spain.

A: You ⁸ _____ from Spain! Where in Spain?

B: I ⁹ _____ from Barcelona.

A: Oh, ¹⁰ _____ from Barcelona, Spain. Nice.

B: Thanks.

A: Are ¹¹ _____ OK?

B: No, ¹² _____ not!

B Put the words in the correct order. Start with the underlined word.

A: ¹I / George / 'm / Hi   *Hi, I'm George.*

B: ²are / from / Where / you?

A: ³'m / Italy / from / I.

B: ⁴from / Are / Rome / you?

A: ⁵I'm / No, / not. ⁶Venice / from / I'm. ⁷you / from / Rome / Are ?

B: ⁸from / I'm / Italy / No, / not. ⁹Ankara, / I'm / Turkey / from / in.

.2 **A** Complete the answers.

1 Where's Saint Petersburg?
   It / Russia.   *It's in Russia.* _____

2 Where's Tripoli?
   It / Libya. _____

3 Where's Shakira from?
   She / Colombia. _____

4 Is Angela Merkel from Germany?
   Yes, / she. _____

5 Is Toyota from China?
   No, / it. / It / Japan. _____

6 Where's Hagia Sophia?
   It / Turkey. _____

7 Is Emma Watson from the USA?
   No, / she. / She / the UK. _____

8 Is Buenos Aires in Brazil?
   No, / it. / It / Argentina. _____

B Complete the questions.

1 ___*Where's*___ Frank?
   He's in New York.

2 _____ Maria _____?
   She's from Spain.

3 _____ Melbourne _____ the USA?
   No, it isn't. It's in Australia.

4 _____ Liverpool?
   It's in the UK.

5 _____ waiter?
   No, he's a customer.

6 _____ teacher?
   No, she's a student.

7 _____ from Germany?
   Yes, it is.

8 _____ Magda?
   She's in Warsaw.

.3 **A** Find and correct the mistakes in the conversation. There are six mistakes.

A: What/your first name?
      's

B: Ana.

A: And what's your surname?

B: I'm Fernandez.

A: And what's you nationality?

B: I'm Italian.

A: And your number phone?

B: It's 0372 952 594.

A: What's email address?

B: It's anastella247@hotmail.com.

A: How you spell 'anastella'? With one 'n'?

B: Yes, one 'n' and two 'l's.

2 LANGUAGE BANK

GRAMMAR

2.1 *be: you/we/they*

positive and negative			
+	You We	're are	students from India. married.*
–	They	aren't are not	

*married = husband and wife

Use *you* for one person or for two, three, four, etc. people.

you   *you*

questions and short answers				
?	Where	are	you/we/they	from?
		Are		in the right room?
	Yes,		you/we/they	are.
	No,			aren't.

Use *be* + subject (*you/we/they*) for questions.

They're married.   *Are they* married?

Use short answers to *yes/no* questions:
Are you students?
Yes, we are. NOT ~~Yes, we're students.~~
Don't use contractions in positive short answers:
Yes, they are. NOT ~~Yes, they're.~~

2.2 possessive adjectives: *my/your/his/her/its/our/their*

subject pronoun	possessive adjective
I	my
you	your
he	his
she	her
it	its
we	our
they	their

Use *your* pens, NOT ~~yours~~ pens.
Use *its* for things and animals.
The café is near here. **Its** *address is 3 Cambridge Street.*
Look at the punctuation:
It's = it is.   *It's* a cat.
Its = possessive:
Its name is Lucky. NOT ~~It's~~ name is Lucky.

My name's Paolo.

Its name's Lucky.

His name's Rob.

Our surname's Romano.

Her name's Ana.

Their names are Sarah and Nick.

2.3 making suggestions

suggestions		response
Let's (Let us)	go. stop. eat.	Good idea. OK. Great.
Let's not	have a coffee. have a break. sit down.	

Use *Let's* + verb to suggest a good idea.
It is a suggestion for you *and* me.
The negative is *Let's not* + verb: *Let's not go.*

PRACTICE

.1

A Change the words in bold to *they, we* or *you*.

1 **Kevin and Nick** are actors.

They're actors.

2 **Michelle and I** are from France.

_____ .

3 **You and Chan** are in the wrong room.

_____ .

4 Are **your mother and father** Brazilian?

_____ ?

5 **My teachers** are Louise and Kerri.

_____ .

6 **Ryan and I** are married.

_____ .

7 **The students** aren't in class.

_____ .

8 A: Where are **you and Jeff**?

_____ ?

B: **Jeff and I** are in class.

_____ .

B Complete the conversation.

A: Hi, where / you / from?

_____ ?

B: We / California.

_____ .

A: you / Los Angeles?

_____ ?

B: No / we / not. We / San Francisco.

_____ .

A: you / Kathy and Chris?

_____ ?

B: No, / they / in Room 205!

_____ .

.2

A Complete the sentences with the words in the box.

| ~~my~~ our (x2) its her their his your (x2) |

my

1 A: Hi, / name's Gina. What's name?

   B: Hi, I'm Brad.

2 A: Who's she?

   B: Oh, name's Julia.

   A: And who's the man with Julia?

   B: I don't know name.

3 A: It's an American sport.

   B: What's name?

   A: American football!

4 A: Mr and Mrs Black, what's phone number?

   B: phone number's 2048 306 8420473.

5 A: This is a photo of children.

   B: What are names?

   A: Jake and Patsy.

B Complete the conversations with the correct subject pronoun (*I/you/he*, etc.) or correct possessive adjective (*my/your/his*, etc.)

Conversation 1

A: Excuse me, is [1]_____ name Black?

B: No, [2]_____ isn't. [3]_____ name's Depp.

A: Are [4]_____ Johnny Depp, the actor?

B: No, [5]_____ 'm not! Please go away!

Conversation 2

A: Where's Angela?

B: [6]_____ isn't here.

A: What's [7]_____ mobile number?

B: Sorry, I don't know.

Conversation 3

A: Are [8]_____ students for the English class?

B: Yes, [9]_____ are. Are you [10]_____ teacher?

A: Yes, [11]_____ am.

.3

A Find and correct the mistakes. There are three mistakes in each conversation.

Conversation 1

A: I'm very tired.

B: OK, ~~let~~ stop now.   *let's*

A: That a good idea.

B: And let's a coffee.

A: No, thanks. I'm not thirsty.

Conversation 2

A: I hungry.

B: I too.

A: Let we eat at the pizzeria.

B: Good idea.

GRAMMAR

3.1 this/that/these/those

	here ↓	there →
singular	this key	that key
plural	these keys	those keys

With *this/that*, use *is*:
*This **is** my book.   That's your book.*
With *these/those*, use *are*:
*These are my DVDs.   Those **are** your DVDs.*

this

that

these

those

3.2 possessive 's

He's	my father's	brother.
They're	my friend's	children.
They're	Rob's	keys.
Is that	Francis's	mobile?
Mariam is	Jalil and Laila's	daughter.
	Catherine's	family name is Hart.

Use 's to show possession.
Use 's with objects: *Rebecca's car, Wei's book.*
Use 's with personal information: *James's email address, Lorenzo's phone number.*
Use 's with family: *Eva's parents, Lucy's brother.*
With two people, put the 's after the second person:
That is Carl and Olga's house.
Note: *Tony's a waiter.* = *Tony is.   I'm Tony's father.* = possessive 's.
Use 's after a word ending in s: *I like Boris's coat.*

3.3 ordering in a café

ordering			
Can I have	a	tea, mineral water, cake,	please?
	two	coffees, colas, sandwiches,	
How much is that?			

taking orders
Can I help you? Anything else? That's £8.

giving alternatives			response
Still		sparkling?	Still, please.
White	or	brown bread?	Brown, please.
Espresso		cappuccino?	Espresso, please.

PRACTICE

.1 **A** Look at the picture and complete the conversation with *this*, *that*, *these* or *those*.

A: Excuse me, is ¹ _this_ your shop?

B: Yes, it is.

A: And is ² _____ your window?

B: Yes. Is ³ _____ your football?

A: No, it's their football.

B: Are ⁴ _____ your children?

A: Yes, ⁵ _____ 's Jerry and ⁶ _____ 's Ed.

B Find and correct the mistakes with *this/that/these/those* in the conversations.

Conversation 1

    These

A: ~~This~~ are our photos of Thailand.

B: Is this your hotel?

A: Yes, it is, and this are our friends, Sanan and Chai.

Conversation 2

A: What's this over there?

B: It's Red Square. And this is your hotel here.

A: Thank you.

Conversation 3

A: What are those in English?

B: They're 'coins'. That one here is a pound coin.

Conversation 4

A: Who are that people over there?

B: That's my brother, Juan and his friends.

Conversation 5

A: Where are those students from?

B: They're from Bogotá, in Colombia.

A: And those student?

B: She isn't a student. She's our teacher!

.2 **A** Write sentences about the family. Use possessive *'s*.

Jon and Ellen

Mark   Sarah

1 Jon is _____*Ellen's*_____ husband.

2 Ellen is _____ mother.

3 Mark is _____ brother.

4 Sarah is _____ sister.

5 Mark is _____ son.

6 Sarah is _____ daughter.

7 Ellen is _____ wife.

8 Jon and Ellen are _____ parents.

B Complete the sentences with possessive *'s*.

1 He's Matt. This is his computer.
   This is _Matt's computer._

2 That's Josh. I'm his friend.
   I'm _____ .

3 She's Emily. Are you her sister?
   Are you _____ ?

4 He's Eric. His surname's White.
   Eric _____ 's White.

5 They're Bella and David. These are their children.
   These are _____ children.

6 This is Rex. His phone number is 396 294.
   _____ is 396 294.

.3 **A** Complete the conversation with the words in the box.

~~you~~ that's have or one can else

      you

A: Can I help /?

B: Yes, can I an egg sandwich, please?

A: White brown bread?

B: Brown, please.

A: Anything?

B: Yes, I have two coffees, please?

A: Espresso or cappuccino?

B: One espresso and cappuccino.

A: OK, seven fifty.

GRAMMAR

4.1   present simple: *I/you/we/they*

positive and negative			
+	I	work	in an office.
	You	have	two children.
−	We	don't like	egg sandwiches.
	They	do not like	

For the negative, use *don't* + verb: *I **don't live** here.*
Don't = do not. Use the contraction *don't* in speaking and informal writing.
Use the present simple to talk about things that are always true.

questions					**short answers**		
?	Do	you/we/they	have	a car?	Yes,	I /we/they	do.
					No,		don't.

***Wh-* questions**			
Where			live?
What	do	you	
When			study?

Use a question word (*what, where*) + do + subject + verb:
Where do you work?

For a question, use *do* + subject + verb.
Do you understand? NOT ~~understand you?~~
In short answers, use
Yes, I do.   No, I don't.
NOT ~~Yes, I understand.   No, I don't understand.~~

4.2   present simple: *he/she/it*

positive and negative			
+	He	likes	children.
	She	goes	to Mexico.
	It	has	an airport.
−	He	doesn't live	in Barcelona.
	She	does not work	in a bank.
	It	doesn't have	a market.

For the negative, use *doesn't* + verb:
*She **doesn't like** chocolate.*
Doesn't = does not. Use the contraction *doesn't* in speaking and informal writing.

spelling rules: present simple: *he/she/it*		
	rule	**example**
most verbs	+ -s	work – he works love – she loves
verbs ending in:		
-ch, -o, -s, -sh, -x	+ -es	teach – he teaches do – she does
consonant + -y	~~y~~ + -ies	study – he studies cry – she cries

Have is irregular: *He **has** a new computer.*

4.3   telling the time

asking the time
What time is it? What time is the film/match/lesson?

telling the time
It's two o'clock. The match is at three o'clock. The party is at three.

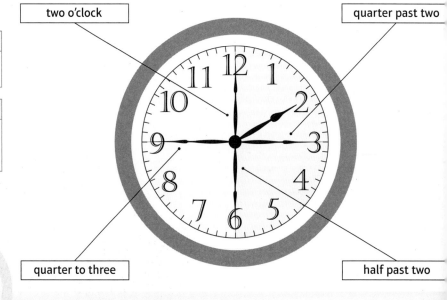

two o'clock

quarter past two

quarter to three

half past two

PRACTICE

.1

A Complete the sentences with the verbs in the box.

| read write eat have know drive like live |

1 I _____don't read_____ newspapers (–)
2 You _____ the colour red. (+)
3 They _____ a sister. (–)
4 We _____ to work. (–)
5 I _____ emails in English. (+)
6 We _____ in Rome. (+)
7 They _____ a lot of cakes! (+)
8 You _____ the answer. (–)

B Put the words in the correct order to make questions.

1 like / Do / children / you?
   Do you like children?
2 and / live / you / Jack / together / Do?
3 you / in / work / Do / an / office?
4 sweater / Do / have / black / you / a?
5 Do / Spanish / understand / parents / your?
6 work / to / walk / you / Do ?

C Complete the short answers for questions 1–6 in Exercise B.

1 Yes, _I do_____.
2 No, _____.
3 Yes, _____.
4 No, _____.
5 Yes, _____.
6 No, _____.

D Write the *Wh-* questions. Use the words in bold to help.

1 _What do you study_____? (you)
   I study **English**.
2 _____? (you)
   We work in **Hong Kong**.
3 _____? (we)
   You have a break **at ten**.
4 _____? (you)
   G-e-o-r-g-e.
5 _____? (they)
   They like **sport and TV**.

.2

A Complete the sentences with the correct form of the verbs in brackets.

1 My mother _____lives_____ in Paris because she
   _____likes_____ cities. (live, like)
2 Rudy _____ me but he _____ me
   every week. (not email, phone)
3 My husband _____ to work or
   he _____. (drive, walk)
4 Lana _____ at home but she _____ it.
   (work, not like)
5 Marco _____ four coffees every day because
   _____ tea. (have, not like)
6 Gina _____ English but she _____ it.
   (understand, not speak)

B Find and correct three mistakes in each conversation.

Conversation 1
A: My wife, Kalila, is a teacher.
B: Near here?
A: Yes, she have a job at City School. She teachs Arabic.
B: Is it a good place to work?
A: Yes, but she don't like the travel every day.

Conversation 2
A: My son Jaime studys engineering at Madrid University.
B: Oh, my daughter gos there. She likes it a lot.
A: Yes, Jaime sais it's good too.

.3

A Write the times in words.

1 _____
2 _____
3 _____
4 _____
5 _____
6 _____
7 _____
8 _____

GRAMMAR

5.1 present simple questions: *he/she/it*

yes/no questions

?	Does	he she it	have	a big breakfast?

short answers

Yes,	he she it	does.
No,		doesn't.

Use *does* + subject + verb for a question.
Does she cook dinner? NOT ~~cooks she dinner?~~
In short answers, use:
Yes, he does.   No, he doesn't.
NOT ~~Yes, she cooks.   No, she doesn't cook.~~

Wh- questions

?	When	does	he she it	get up?
	What time			have breakfast?
	Where			live?
	What			do?

Use a question word (*what, where, what time, when*) + *does* + subject + verb:
When does she eat?
What does he do? = *What's his job?*

5.2 adverbs of frequency

positive and negative

+	I/You/We	always	work	on Sundays.
	He/She	usually often sometimes never	has	a coffee.
–	I/You/We	don't usually	cook	breakfast.
	He/She	doesn't often	have	

Adverbs of frequency go **before** most verbs:
I sometimes write emails in English.
Adverbs of frequency go **after** *don't/doesn't*:
I don't often work at the weekend.

adverbs of frequency with *be*

+	I	'm	always	hungry.
	It	's	usually	here.
–	She	isn't	often	

Adverbs of frequency go **after** the verb *be*:
I'm often tired.
Use adverbs of frequency to say how often we do activities
I always do my homework.
He doesn't often play tennis.

never	not often	sometimes	often	usually	alway
0%	10%	40%	60%	80%	100%

5.3 asking for information

questions

What time When	does	the tour	leave?
		the café	open?
	is	lunch?	
How much	does	it	cost?
	is	it?	

responses

It opens	at nine. from 6a.m. to 10p.m. every day except Monday.
It closes It leaves	at two o'clock. at half past nine.
It costs It's	twenty euros.

PRACTICE

.1

A Put the words in the correct order to make questions.

1 live / Does / here / Patrizia?
Does Patrizia live here?
2 Chinese / Stefan / Does / speak?
3 Katia / Does / children / have?
4 your / like / job / brother / his / Does?
5 a / cat / have / Does / name / your?
6 word / this / Does / mean / 'very big'?

B Complete the answers with *does* or *doesn't*.

a) Yes, she ____*does*____. In flat five.
b) Yes, she _____. A son and a daughter.
c) No, it _____. It means 'very good'.
d) Yes, he _____, but he works from eight to seven.
e) No, he _____, but he speaks Japanese.
f) Yes, it _____. Its name is Fluffy.

C Match questions 1–6 with answers a)–f).

1b)

D Complete the questions. Use the words in brackets.

Conversation 1
A: Where [1] ___*does your brother live*___? (your brother)
B: He lives in Copenhagen.
A: Where [2] _____? (he)
B: He works in a school.

Conversation 2
A: What time [3] _____? (Cristina)
B: She gets home at half past four.
A: And when [4] _____? (she)
B: She has dinner at six o'clock.

Conversation 3
A: What [5] _____? ('late')
B: It means after the correct time.
A: Oh. And what time [6] _____?
   (the lesson)
B: It starts at 9a.m.

.2

A Complete the sentences. Use the words in brackets.

1 I do sport. (never)
I never do sport.
2 My mother phones me on Monday evenings. (usually)
3 He's tired in the mornings. (often)
4 We have a drink after work on Fridays. (always)
5 Do you walk to work? (usually)
6 I'm at home in the afternoons. (not usually)
7 Classes are on Saturdays. (sometimes)
8 I watch TV. (not often)

B Look at the chart and complete the conversation. Use adverbs of frequency.

	Mon	Tue	Wed	Thu	Fri	Sat	Sun
vegetables							
fruit							✓
chicken	✓		✓		✓	✓	
steak	✓	✓	✓	✓	✓	✓	✓
fish		✓		✓			
chips	✓	✓	✓		✓	✓	✓

A: So, Mr Price, let's look at your diet. Do you eat vegetables and fruit?
B: Er, no, doctor. I ____*never*____ ____*eat*____ vegetables and I _____ _____ _____ fruit.
A: What about meat and fish?
B: Well, I _____ _____ fish, maybe once or twice a week and I _____ _____ chicken. I like steak so I _____ _____ steak for lunch and I _____ _____ it with chips.

.3

A Complete the conversation with the words in the box.

~~me~~ do to it does what opens except

A: Excuse /*me*/?

B: Can I help you?

A: Yes, time is dinner?

B: From seven half past ten.

A: And you have a swimming pool?

B: Yes, it opens every day Sunday.

A: When it open?

B: It at seven in the morning.

A: When does close?

B: I closes at nine in the evening.

GRAMMAR

6.1 there is/are

positive and negative				
+	There	's	a restaurant	in the station. here. near here. over there.
		is	a café	
		are	payphones	
–	There	isn't	a hotel	
		aren't	any cafés	

Use *There's* (*There is*) + singular noun: **There's a chair** here.
Use *There are* + plural noun: **There are** two **chairs** here.
Use *There's* (*There is*) and *There are* to say something exists:
There's a Spanish class for beginners.
= *The school has a Spanish class for beginners.*
Use *There's* (*There is*) and *There are* to talk about places, and things or people in places:
There's a gym in the hotel. = *The hotel has a gym.*

questions			short answers		
Is	there	a cash machine here?	Yes,	there	is.
			No,		isn't.
Are	there	any shops in the station?	Yes,	there	are.
			No,		aren't.

To make a question:

There's a pharmacy.   **Is there** a pharmacy?
Use short answers to *yes/no* questions:
Is there a café? Yes, **there is**. NOT ~~Yes, there is a café.~~
Use *Is there a/an* + singular noun / *Are* + *there* + (*any*) + plural noun for *yes/no* questions.
With plural nouns, use *any* in the question form and the negative:
Are there **any** *shops? There aren't* **any** *shops.*

6.2 a/an, some, a lot of, not any

a/an

Use *a/an* + singular noun for one thing or person.
Use *a* before consonants (*b, c, d, f,* etc.) and *an* before vowels (*a, e, i, o, u*):
There's **a p**roblem.   *Can I have* **an e**gg sandwich?

some

Use *some* + plural noun for a small number of things or people:
I have **some sweets** *in my bag.*

a lot of

Use *a lot of* + plural noun for a large number of things or people:
Are there **a lot of students** *in your class?*

not any

Use *not any* + plural noun for zero (0):
I don't have **any bananas**.   *There aren't* **any buses**.
Also use *no* + noun for zero: *I have* **no bananas**.   *There are* **no buses**.

6.3 buying a ticket

asking for a ticket	
A single	to Cairo, please.
A return	to Moscow for
Two singles	tomorrow, please.
A monthly pass	to Central Station, please.

asking for information		
Which	gate platform	is it?
What time When	's	the first bus? the next bus? the last bus?
	is	
	does it arrive	in Sydney?

giving information		
What time When	do you want	to go? to come back?
There's	a bus one	at four.
The train	leaves from	platform 2.
The bus		gate 21.

PRACTICE

.1

A Look at the picture and read the sentences. Write sentences beginning with *There's, There are, There isn't* or *There aren't*.

1 *There's a book*   , so I think the woman likes reading.
2 There's a ticket, so I think she likes the cinema.
3 There're bags, so she works in a bank.
4 There aren't ou, so she doesn't have a car.
5 There's ri, so she's married.
6 here, so she doesn't have good eyes.
7 there, so she likes cats.
8 There, so maybe she doesn't have any children.

B Complete the conversations with the words in the box.

| Is there   aren't   there (x2)   are (x3) |
| there's   isn't   Are   is (x2) |

Conversation 1
A: [1]   *Is there*   a wallet on the table?
B: No, there [2] isn't , but [3] there's a bag.

Conversation 2
A: Excuse me, [4] are [5] there any toilets near here?
B: Yes, there [6] are men's and women's toilets over there.

Conversation 3
A: [7] Are there any night buses?
B: No, there [8] aren't, but there [9] are taxis.

Conversation 4
A: Excuse me, [10] is [11] there a doctor here?
B: Yes, there [12] is . Dr Mantel.

.2

A Look at the picture and complete the sentences with *There's/are* and *a/an, some, a lot of* or *n't (not) any*.

1 *There's a*   phone.
2 There're a photos.
3 There isn't a computer.
4 There's an apple.
5 There a lot of pens.
6 There aren't a keys.

B Put the words in order to make sentences.

1 have / lot / money / Students / a / of / don't   students don't have a lot money
2 a / pages / has / lot / book / A / usually / of   A book usually has a lot of pages
3 have / Some / don't / people / home / a   Some people don't
4 any / but / sister / Ben / have / has / brothers / he / doesn't / a
5 of / Our / has / lot / students / school / a   our school has a lot
6 a / of / Some / have / lot / children / people

.3

A Complete the conversation with the words in the box.

| ~~singles~~   a   's   gate   do   it   from   tomorrow |

singles

A: Two singles to Glasgow, please.

B: For today?

A: Sorry, no, for. tomorrow

B: When you want to go?

A: At about nine o'clock in the morning.

B: OK, that's seven pounds fifty.

A: What time the bus?

B: There's one at quarter to nine.

A: When does arrive in Glasgow?

B: At half past nine.

A: Which is it?   gate

B: It leaves number 22.

A: Thanks lot.

GRAMMAR

7.1   past simple: *was/were*

positive and negative				
+	I/He/She/It	was	here	yesterday.
	You/We/They	were	at work	on Friday.
−	I/He/She/It	wasn't	tired	this morning.
	You/We/They	weren't		

questions				short answers			
?	Was	I/he/she/it	OK? right?	Yes, No,	I/he/she/it	was. wasn't.
	Were	you/we/they	here?	Yes No,	you/we/they	were. weren't.

The past simple of *be* is *was/were*.
Use *was/were* to talk about the past:
*It **was** cold last week.*
Add *n't* (*not*) for the negative: *wasn't* = *was not*,
weren't = *were not*.
Use contractions in speaking and informal writing:
*We **weren't** at home yesterday.*

Wh- questions with *was/were*		
Where	was	your party?
When	were	the last Olympic Games?

Use *was/were* + subject (*I, you*) for questions:

She was in Spain.   ***Was she** in Spain?*

You were at school together.   ***Were you** at school together?*

Use short answers to *yes/no* questions:
*Was it good? Yes, **it was**.* NOT ~~Yes, it was good~~.

Use *Wh-* question words + *was/were* + subject to ask questions in the past:
What was the problem?

7.2   past simple: regular verbs

positive and negative			
+	I/You/He/She/It/We/They	worked	yesterday.
		closed	at four.
		studied	all weekend.
		stopped	last week.
−		didn't wait. did not start.	

spellings: regular past simple verbs		
	rule	**example**
most verbs	+ *-ed*	work – worked
verbs ending in:		
-e	+ *-d*	close – closed
consonant + *-y*	~~y~~ + *-ied*	try – tried
consonant-vowel-consonant	double the final consonant + *-ed*	travel – travelled

Note: *opened, listened* NOT ~~openned, listenned~~

The past simple is the same for *I/You/He/She/It/We/They*.
In the negative, use *didn't* + verb:
*I **didn't wait**.* NOT *I ~~didn't waited~~*.
Use the contraction *didn't* in speaking and informal writing.

Use the past simple to talk about:
• something which happened at a point in the past:
*We **arrived** at three o'clock.*

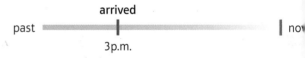
past | arrived | now
3p.m.

• something which started and finished in the past:
*We **played** tennis for three hours.*

past | played | now
9a.m.   12p.m.

7.3   asking for and giving opinions

asking for opinions		
How	is was were	the food? the party? the people?
What	do you think of	

giving opinions		
It	's/was	delicious.
They	're/were	lovely. great.
It	wasn't	fantastic. good. boring. very good.

Use *I think* with opinions:
I think it's very good.

PRACTICE

7.1 **A** Complete the sentences with the correct form of *be* in the present or the past.

1 I _____ '*m* _____ (+) here now but I _____ *wasn't* _____ (–) here yesterday.

2 He _____ (–) at home today, but he _____ (+) at home yesterday.

3 The shops _____ (–) open yesterday, but they _____ (+) open today.

4 We _____ (+) all tired yesterday, but we _____ (–) tired today.

5 She _____ (–) at work yesterday, but she _____ (+) at work today.

6 You _____ (+) relaxed today, but you _____ (–) relaxed yesterday.

B Add words to make questions about the past. Then write the short answers.

1 James / here / this morning? ✗
   Was James here this morning? _____ *No, he wasn't.* _____

2 the film / good? ✓
   _____? _____.

3 your brothers and sisters / nice to you? ✓
   _____? _____.

4 you / cold / in Scotland? ✗
   _____? _____.

5 you and Emma / at the party? ✗
   _____? _____.

6 there / a gift shop / in the hotel? ✓
   _____? _____.

7.2 **A** Write the sentences in the past simple with the words in brackets.

1 The shop opens at ten. (Yesterday / nine)
   Yesterday the shop opened at nine.

2 My father plays golf at the weekend. (Last weekend / tennis)
   Last weekend my father played tenni

3 Francisco works in a bank. (Last year / shop)
   Last year Francisco worked in shop

4 I study English a lot. (Last night / all night)
   Last night I studied English all night

5 My parents often move home. (In 2009 / to Barcelona)
   In 2009 my parents moved to Barcelona

6 The train stops for a quarter of an hour. (Yesterday / half an hour)
   Yesterday the train stopped for half an hour

B Add words to make sentences. Use the correct form of the past simple.

1 In 2010 / we / live / in London, but / we / not / like / it.
   In 2010 we lived in London, but we didn't like it.

2 Noriko / email / me yesterday, but she / not / phone.

3 The film / not / start / until eight, and / it / finish / at eleven.

4 James / want / to see the concert, but he / arrive / an hour late.

5 I / repeat / the instructions because / the students / not / understand.

6 I try / to phone you last night, but you / not answer.

7.3 **A** Find and correct the mistakes. There are four mistakes in each conversation.

Conversation 1

A: Hi, Sally. ~~Who~~ How was the film?

B: It was delicious, really great.

A: Who was in it?

B: Tom Hanks.

A: How is he?

B: Was fantastic!

Conversation 2

A: Where do you think of the chicken?

B: It's very good – really awful.

A: Oh, I'm sorry.

B: Who's your steak?

A: I'm think it's OK.

B: And this restaurant is very expensive.

A: Yes, it is!

GRAMMAR

8.1 past simple: irregular verbs

+	I/You/We/They/He/She/It	went	to South Africa.
		had	a coffee.
		met	a lot of people.

−	I/You/We/They/He/She/It	didn't	go	on holiday.
			have	breakfast.
			meet	our friends.

Many common verbs have an irregular past simple form.
The negative form is the same for regular and
irregular verbs:
I didn't go to work yesterday. NOT ~~I didn't went to work yesterday.~~
She didn't have lunch. NOT ~~She didn't had lunch.~~

Irregular verb list

present	past	present	past
be	was/were	have	had
become	became	know	knew
break	broke	meet	met
come	came	put	put
do	did	say	said
drive	drove	see	saw
eat	ate	sit	sat
get	got	take	took
go	went	think	thought
give	gave	write	wrote

8.2 past simple: questions

yes/no questions					short answers		
?	Did	I/you/he/she/it/we/they	start	in New York?	Yes,	I/you/he/she/it/we/they	did.
			go	to Paris?	No,		didn't.

Use *Did* + subject + verb for a question.
Did you start? NOT ~~Did you started?~~   *Did you go?* NOT ~~Did you went?~~
The question form is the same for regular and irregular verbs.
In short answers, use:
Yes, I did./No, I didn't. NOT ~~Yes, I started. No, I didn't go.~~

Wh- questions			
When			
Where	did	you	go?
Why			
How			
What	did	you	do?
Who	did	you	meet?

The question word comes before *did*.

8.3 giving directions

asking for directions		
	where's	the fruit?
Excuse me,	where are	the DVDs?
	is there	a post office near here?

giving directions		
Do you see	the vegetables?	
	the shop over there?	
The fruit	is	next to the vegetables.
The DVDs	are	opposite the magazines.
		on the right.
		near the yoghurts.
There	's	a post office over there.

To check instructions, use: *Let me check* or *Can I check?*

PRACTICE

.1

A Complete the sentences with the correct form of the verb in bold.

1 They didn't **come** to class on Monday but they ____came____ on Tuesday.

2 He **took** a taxi, he didn't _____ a bus.

3 You **said** hello, but you didn't _____ your name.

4 She didn't **think** the film was good but he _____ it was great.

5 I didn't **become** a nurse, I _____ a doctor.

6 We didn't **sit** here, we _____ over there.

B Complete the story with the past form of the verbs in the box.

~~meet~~ break drive go have (x2) give
see become not have eat

I ¹____met____ my wife Manuela one weekend on a mountain in Scotland. On that Saturday morning the weather was good and I ²_____ out at eight o'clock. But around two o'clock the weather ³_____ very bad. At five o'clock I was lost, cold, and very hungry. Then I ⁴_____ someone on the mountain. It was Manuela. She ⁵_____ any food but she ⁶_____ some chocolate and some water. She ⁷_____ the chocolate in two and ⁸_____ me half. We ⁹_____ the chocolate and talked. Then she helped me down the mountain. She ¹⁰_____ a car and she ¹¹_____ me back to my hotel. I asked her to dinner and that was the beginning of our story.

.2

A Complete the conversations with the past form of the verbs in brackets.

1 A: ____Did____ you ____leave____ home at six in the morning? (leave)
  B: Yes, we ____did____. But the plane ____left____ at six in the evening!

2 A: _____ you _____ David at school? (meet)
  B: No, I _____. We _____ last year at work.

3 A: _____ you _____ in the film? (cry)
  B: Yes, I _____. I _____ a lot.

4 A: _____ you _____ Mike yesterday afternoon? (see)
  B: No, I _____, but I _____ him in the morning.

5 A: _____ you _____ this email? (write)
  B: Yes, I _____. I _____ it yesterday. Is there a problem?

6 A: _____ you _____ a good time in Uruguay? (have)
  B: Yes, we _____. We _____ a fantastic time, thanks.

B Write questions about the underlined information.

1 I met an old friend.
  Who did you meet?

2 We went to a restaurant.
  _____

3 We ate pizza.
  _____

4 We drank mineral water.
  _____

5 We watched a film.
  _____

6 I came home at midnight.
  _____

.3

A Find and correct the mistakes in the conversation. There are six mistakes.

A: Excuse me, where ~~is~~ *are* the sweets?

B: Are you see the newspapers over there?

A: Where?

B: Over there, near of the snacks.

A: Oh, yes.

B: Well, the sweets are next the newspapers, on the right.

A: Can I check? They're the left of the newspapers.

B: No, they're on right.

A: Ah, yes. Thanks a lot.

B: No problem.

GRAMMAR

9.1 object pronouns

subject pronouns	object pronouns
I	me
you	you
he	him
she	her
it	it
we	us
they	them

Subject pronouns go **before** the verb.
Object pronouns go **after** the verb.
*Karen loves cats but I hate **them**.*
Don't repeat nouns and noun phrases. Use a pronoun:
*Megan's brother is a doctor and I like ~~Megan's brother~~ **him** very much.*
A: *Do you know Amelia?*
B: *No, I don't know ~~Amelia~~ **her**.*
After prepositions, use nouns or object pronouns:
*Listen **to the teacher/to me**.*
*I went to the cinema **with friends/with them**.*

9.2 like, love, hate + -ing

positive and negative

+	I/You/We/They	like/love/hate	cats.
	He/She/It	likes/loves/hates	computer games. going to parties. them.
−	I/You/We/They	don't like	
	He/She/It	doesn't like	

Be careful with the short answers:
Do you like playing tennis? *Yes I do.* NOT ~~*Yes, I like.*~~
  No, I don't. NOT ~~*No, I don't like.*~~
To talk about your feelings:
• use *love/(don't) like/hate* + plural noun: *I love apples.*
• use *love/(don't) like/hate* + verb + *-ing*: *I hate driving.*

spellings: -ing forms

	rule	example
most verbs	+ *-ing*	go – going study – studying
verbs ending in:		
-e	*~~e~~* + *-ing*	phone – phoning drive – driving
consonant-vowel-consonant	double the final consonant + *-ing*	get – getting sit – sitting

9.3 making requests

I/He/She etc.	'd like	two coffees, please.
	would like	a new computer.
Can I	see	that one?
Can you	help	me?

Use *would like* + noun = *Can I have* or *I want*.
Would like is polite.
Note:
I'd like a banana. = I want a banana now.
I like bananas. = I always like bananas.

asking what someone wants

					response
	Would	you	like	a drink?	Yes, please. No, thanks/Thank you.
	Do		want		
What	would	you	like?		I'd like a cola, please.
Which one					

To ask what someone wants, use *Do you want* + noun or *Would you like* + noun?
Would you like is more polite.

PRACTICE

.1

A Find and correct the mistakes in the sentences. Two sentences are correct.

1 Leo and Irena were here yesterday. I had lunch with ~~her~~. *them*

2 That's your sister's toy. Give it to him.

3 Deena lived with we for three years.

4 I love this music. Come and dance with I.

5 I spoke to Muhammed last night and asked him about it.

6 These apples aren't very good. I don't like these.

7 When did I first talk to you?

8 Andy's good at tennis. I played with he yesterday.

9 Diana's in my class. I like she a lot.

10 The exit is over there, in front of your.

B Look at the conversations. Complete B's parts with an object pronoun.

1 A: Did you see John yesterday?
   B: Yes I saw /\ at lunch.   *him*

2 A: How was the chicken?
   B: I didn't like.

3 A: Do you have the tickets?
   B: Oh, no! I put in my other coat.

4 A: You're very late!
   B: Sorry, I sent you a text. Did you get?

5 A: Where's Alex?
   B: He phoned this morning from home. He isn't well.

6 A: Was Jennifer at the party?
   B: No, I asked but she didn't want to go.

7 A: How did you and Al get to your hotel?
   B: A taxi met at the airport.

8 A: Thank you Mr Abaasi.
   B: Wait a minute, class. Did I give your homework?

.2

A Write the *-ing* form of the verbs.

1 be _____being_____
2 chat _____
3 work _____
4 write _____
5 say _____
6 have _____
7 start _____
8 stop _____
9 cook _____
10 email _____

B Add words to make two conversations.

Conversation 1
A: you / like / do / sport?   *Do you like doing sport?*
B: Well, / like / swim / but I / not / like / run.
A: you / like / play / tennis?
B: Yes, / I.

Conversation 2
A: Sam / not / like / speak / on the phone.
B: he / like / write / emails?
A: No, he / but / he / love / meet / people / online.
B: And / he / like / play / computer games?
A: Yes, / he.

.3

A Complete the conversations with the words in the box.

| ~~Can~~ like I thanks I'd have Would 'd |

Conversation 1
A: [1]_____Can_____ I help you?
B: Yes, please. I [2]_____ like one of those shirts.
B: OK. Which colour would you [3]_____?
A: Um … Can I [4]_____ the red one, please?

Conversation 2
A: Can [5]_____ get you a drink?
B: Er … Yes, [6]_____ like a tea please.
A: [7]_____ you like some sugar?
B: No, [8]_____.

GRAMMAR

10.1 can/can't

positive and negative			
+	I/You/He/She/It/We/They	can	swim.
–		can't	play tennis.

questions			short answers		
Can	I/you/he/she/it/we/they	drive?	Yes,	I/he/she/it/we/they	can.
		cook Mexican food?	No,		can't.

Use *can/can't* + verb: *I can dance.* NOT ~~I can to dance~~.

Use short answers to *yes/no* questions: *Can you sing? Yes, I* **can***./No, I* **can't**. NOT ~~Yes, I can swim./No, I can't swim.~~

Use *can* + subject (*you, he*) for questions.

*He can play tennis.   **Can he** play tennis?*

Use *can* or *can't* to talk about ability. You know how to do something.

Use *very well, well, quite well, not very well* with *can*:

*I can swim **very well**.* (✔✔✔)
*I can sing **well**.* (✔✔)
*I can cook **quite well**.* (✔)
*I can speak English, but **not very well**.* (–)
*I **can't** drive.* (✗)

10.2 be going to

positive and negative				
+	I	'm		get fit.
	He/She/It	's	going to	
	You/We/They	're		
–	I	'm not		lose weight.
	He/She/It	isn't		
	You/We/They	aren't		

Use *be going to* + verb to talk about future plans.

Am	I		meet new people?
Is	he/she/it	going to	learn something new?
Are	you/we/they		

Use *be* + subject + *going to* + verb for questions.

Yes, I'm going to go on a diet. But not today!

lose weight

past | —————— | —————— | —————— | future
                        now

10.3 starting/ending conversations

starting conversations	ending conversations
This is a great/nice place.	Is that the time?
Excuse me, do you have the time?	I'm sorry. I can see an old friend over there.
What do you think of the music/food/party?	Nice to talk to you/meet you.
So are you from around here?	I hope we meet again.

PRACTICE

0.1 **A** Complete the sentences with the verb in brackets and the correct form of *can*.

1 Help, help! _____*I can't swim*_____! (swim)
2 Excuse me, _____ English? (speak)
3 Martin _____ a horse, but not very well. (ride)
4 I'm sorry. I _____ your name. (remember)
5 Rita _____ very good photos so let's ask her. (take)
6 These words are very small. _____ them for me? (read)
7 I _____ the game of chess. (never understand)
8 I don't have my glasses with me so I _____ very well. (see)

B Complete the conversation with *can* (x4) and *can't* (x4).

A: Are you OK? _{Can} you stand up?

B: Let me try. Yes, I.

A: you walk on it?

B: I don't know. Oh no, I.

A: OK, just sit down and relax.

B: I relax! Where's my mobile?

A: I see it. You use my mobile.

B: It's no good. I get a phone signal here. you go and get help?

0.2 **A** Find and correct the mistakes in the sentences 1–8. There are mistakes in six of the sentences.

1 I ^{'m}/going to see Juan this afternoon.

2 I are going to stay at home tomorrow.

3 Is Charlotte going be a writer?

4 We aren't going to arrive before seven o'clock.

5 Antonio going to leave work at five.

6 Are you going pay?

7 Kiera and Sam is going to drive to Chicago.

8 My daughter isn't going to sell her flat.

B Complete the conversation with the words in the box. You do **not** need to use one of the words.

| ~~'m~~ not buy going are go to is he |

A: I ¹_____'m_____ going to get up early tomorrow and go running. Do you want to come?
B: No, I'm going ²_____ stay up late tonight, so I'm ³_____ going to get up early tomorrow.
A: Oh, is there something good on TV?
B: No, it's my father's fiftieth birthday and ⁴_____'s going to have a party.
A: Oh, that's right. ⁵_____ you going to give him a new mobile phone?
B: No, I'm going to ⁶_____ him a GPS for his car. Do you want to come and help me choose one?
A: Sorry, I can't. Celia's here.
B: Oh, ⁷_____ she going to help you with your computer?
A: Yes, that's right.
B: OK. I'm ⁸_____ to go to the shop now. See you later.

0.3 **A** Put the words in bold in the correct order.

Conversation 1
A: Excuse me, ¹**the / you / time / do / have**?
Do you have the time?
B: Yes, it's half past eight.
A: ²**nice / is / place / a / This**.
B: It's OK. ³**you / What / of / music / do / think / the**?
A: It's great.

Conversation 2
A: I'm sorry, ⁴**old / there / friend / can / see / an / over / I**.
B: Oh, right.
A: ⁵**you / talk / to / Nice / to**.
B: You too. ⁶**we / again / hope / I / meet**.

Conversation 3
A: ⁷**that / time / Is / the**? Oh, no!
B: What's the problem?
A: ⁸**minutes / meeting / in / ten / a / have / I**.
B: OK. Goodbye.
A: Bye.

PHOTO BANK

1 A Match the words with photos A–N.

1 bank
2 camera
3 cinema
4 computer
5 email
6 information
7 internet
8 pizza
9 restaurant
10 supermarket
11 taxi
12 television/TV
13 tennis
14 university

B Are the words the same in your language?

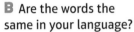

Lead-in **CLASSROOM LANGUAGE**

1 Match the verbs and expressions with pictures A–L.

1 answer   *H*
2 ask
3 listen
4 read
5 write
6 look
7 circle
8 tick
9 underline
10 work alone
11 work in pairs
12 check your answers

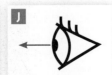

Lesson 1.1 COUNTRIES AND NATIONALITIES

1 A Match the countries with the flags.

1 Spain *A*
2 Argentina
3 Mexico
4 Poland
5 Australia
6 Japan
7 India
8 Chile

B Cover the countries above and complete the table with the correct countries.

Nationality	Country	Nationality	Country
-an /-ian		*-ese*	
1 American		9 Chinese	
2 Argentinian		10 Japanese	
3 Colombian		*-ish*	
4 German		11 British	
5 Italian		12 Polish	
6 Chilean		13 Spanish	
7 Mexican		14 Turkish	
8 Russian			

Lesson 1.2 JOBS

1 A Match the jobs with photos A–J.

1 a cleaner *F*
2 a cook/chef
3 a hotel manager
4 a nurse
5 an office worker
6 a police officer
7 a receptionist
8 retired
9 a shop assistant
10 a tourist information assistant

B Put the jobs in the correct group.

a sportsman   an actor   a businesswoman
a waitress   an actress   a waiter
a sportswoman   a businessman

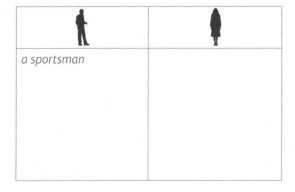

a sportsman	

PHOTO BANK

Lesson 2.3 FEELINGS

1 A Match the adjectives with photos A–H.

1 angry	5 scared/afraid
2 happy	6 surprised
3 ill	7 unhappy
4 interested	8 well/fine

B Are the adjectives good (+) or bad (–)? Complete the table.

+	–
happy	

C Cover Exercises A and B and practice alone or with another student. Point to a picture and say the sentence.

He's angry. She's ill.

Lesson 3.1 OBJECTS

1 A Match the names of the objects with the photos A–J.

1 a bag	6 a business card
2 a credit card	7 a newspaper
3 a picture	8 a clock
4 a dictionary	9 a pencil
5 a glass	10 a watch

B Work in pairs. Which objects are in the classroom?

   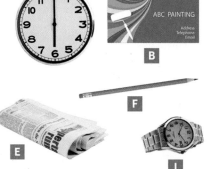

2 A Write the plurals of the words in Exercise 1A in the correct place.

most words	+ -s	key – key**s**	pens
after -x, -ss, -sh, -ch	+ -es	box – box**es**	
after consonant + -y	y̶ + -ies	city – cit**ies**	

a boy

B Write the words in the box under the photos.

a boy a man children girls
boys a woman a girl men
a child women

Lesson 3.2 COLOURS AND CLOTHES

1 Match the names of the clothes with the photos A–J.

1 a coat
2 a dress
3 trousers
4 a skirt
5 a T-shirt
6 a tie
7 trainers
8 gloves
9 glasses
10 socks

A

B

C

D

E

F

H

I

J

2 Write words 1–10 under the colours.

1 black
2 blue
3 brown
4 green
5 orange
6 pink
7 purple
8 red
9 white
10 yellow

A

B

C

D

E

F

G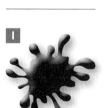

H

I

J

PHOTO BANK

Lesson 4.1 VERB PHRASES

1 A Write verbs 1–8 under the photos.

1 be
2 cost
3 listen
4 play
5 read
6 write
7 watch
8 want

_be_ a teacher

_____ a newspaper

_____ to music

_____ guita

_____ ten euros

_____ TV

_____ an email

_____ a car

B Complete the word webs with a verb from 1–8 in Exercise 1A.

a new job
a) ___want___
a big TV
a DVD
e) _____
a film

twenty-eight
b) _____
hungry
tennis
f) _____
golf

to the teacher
c) _____
to the radio
a lot
g) _____
five dollars

a book
d) _____
the news online
a blog
h) _____
a text

Lesson 4.3 TIMES

1 Write the time under the clocks.

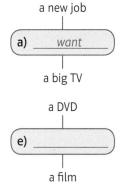

five past eight

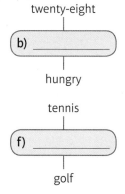

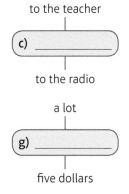

twenty-five to ten

Lesson 5.1 DAILY ROUTINES: MOVEMENT VERBS

1 Match phrases 1–4 with pictures A–D.

1 get home
2 go to work
3 come home
4 leave home

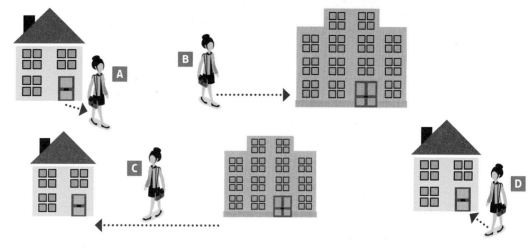

2 A Complete the word webs with a verb in the box.

~~have~~ go make
get leave
start/finish

B Work in pairs and take turns. Cover the word webs. Student A: say a verb from the box. Student B: say three verb phrases.

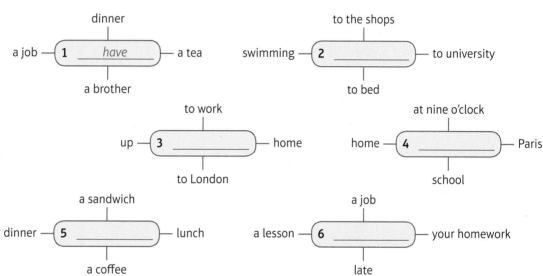

dinner
a job — **1** ___have___ — a tea
a brother

to the shops
swimming — **2** _____ — to university
to bed

to work
up — **3** _____ — home
to London

at nine o'clock
home — **4** _____ — Paris
school

a sandwich
dinner — **5** _____ — lunch
a coffee

a job
a lesson — **6** _____ — your homework
late

Lesson 5.2 FOOD

1 A Match the names of the food with photos A–L.

1 apples
2 carrots
3 bread
4 tomatoes
5 orange juice
6 lettuce
7 milk
8 peppers
9 potatoes
10 bananas
11 cereal
12 oil

B Cross out the item in each group that does not belong.

1 apple, orange, pepper, banana
2 cereal, potato, carrot, tomato
3 oil, orange juice, milk, bread

PHOTO BANK

1 Match the places with photos A–P.

1 an airport O
2 a bank H
3 a cinema J
4 a factory F
5 a farm B
6 a gym A
7 a hospital C
8 a library N
9 a museum P
10 a park L
11 a post office D
12 a school G
13 a shopping centre I
14 a supermarket K
15 a theatre M
16 a zoo E

1 Match the signs with photos A–J.

1 danger – keep out
2 entrance
3 fire exit
4 look both ways
5 no entry
6 no smoking
7 pull
8 push
9 toilets (Ladies, Gentlemen)
10 way out

Lesson 7.1 DATES: YEARS

1 Match 1–8 with A–H.

1 nineteen eighty-four *E*
2 two thousand and one
3 nineteen ninety-nine
4 sixteen twenty-three
5 two thousand and eight
6 eighteen fifty
7 nineteen forty-five
8 twenty twenty

A 2001 **B** 1945 **C** 1623
D 2008 **E** 1984 **F** 2020
G 1850 **H** 1999

Lesson 7.1 DATES: TIME PHRASES

1 Match the time phrases with the days/dates/times.

1 last month
2 last night
3 last week
4 last weekend
5 last year
6 yesterday morning
7 yesterday evening
8 on Tuesday afternoon

a) Saturday 13 June–Sunday 14 June
b) Thursday 18 June, 6a.m.–12 noon
c) Thursday 18 June, 10p.m.–6a.m.
d) Thursday 18 June, 6p.m.–10p.m.
e) May
f) Tuesday 16 June, 1p.m.–6p.m.
g) Monday 8 June–Sunday 14 June
h) 2014

TODAY
FRIDAY
19
JUNE 2015

Lesson 7.3 ADJECTIVES

1 A Match the adjectives with photos A–I.

1 far _____E_____ _____near_____
2 soft _____ _____
3 heavy _____ _____
4 dark _____ _____
5 long _____ _____
6 full _____ _____
7 expensive _____ _____
8 noisy _____ _____
9 fast _____ _____

B Write the words in the box next to the opposites above.

short ~~near~~ light (x2) quiet
slow cheap hard empty

A

B

C

D

E Santiago 2500 KM

F

G

H

I

PHOTO BANK

Lesson 8.1   PREPOSITIONS OF PLACE

1 A Look at the photos. Complete the sentences with the prepositions in the box.

in   under   at   on (x2)   over

1 The cat's _____ the table.

2 There's a man _____ a car.

3 There's a plane _____ the sea.

4 There are two elephants _____ a river.

5 I live _____ number sixty-six.

6 Rome is _____ the River Tiber.

B Correct one mistake in each sentence.

1 I live in a flat under Beijing.

2 We flew at the Red Desert and arrived in Sydney at 7.

3 They sat over the big tree in the park.

4 To go to the airport, wait for the bus in gate 15.

5 Your keys are in the table in the hall.

6 Our house is over the main road to the city.

Lesson 8.2   THE WEATHER

1 A Match the weather in 1–6 with photos A–F.

1 It was cold.   *F*
2 It was hot and sunny.
3 It was cloudy.
4 It was windy.
5 It rained.
6 It snowed.

B Write answers to the questions.

How was the weather:

1 yesterday?
2 last weekend?
3 on your last holiday?
4 on your last birthday?

Lesson 9.1   MONEY

1 A Match the words with photos A–H.

1 cash
2 a cash machine
3 change
4 a cheque
5 a coin
6 a credit card
7 a note
8 a receipt

B Work in pairs and discuss. Which things do you have in your bag now?

Lesson 9.2 ACTIVITIES

1 A Match the activities with photos A–H.

1 clean your teeth
2 draw a picture
3 get dressed
4 have a shower
5 use a computer
6 send a text
7 sign a letter
8 turn on the radio

B Work in pairs and discuss. Which of the activities do you …

… do every day?
… like doing?
… never do?

Lesson 10.1 ABILITY VERBS

1 Match the sentences with photos A–J.

1 He can't reach it.
2 He can't lift it.
3 She can climb.
4 He can throw it.
5 He can't catch.
6 He can't type.
7 She can paint.
8 She can run.
9 She can't hear.
10 She can jump.

COMMUNICATION BANK

Lesson 1.2

6 A Student A: write two *yes/no* questions about each photo A–C. Ask about jobs and places.

Photo A: Is she a singer? Is she from the USA?   Photo C: Is it in Russia?

Kenji is from Japan. He's an actor.

Fatima is an engineer from Libya.

It's the city of Florence, in Italy.

B Ask Student B your questions about photos A–C.

C Listen to Student B and answer questions about photos D–F.

Lesson 1.3

2 A Student A: read the letters below to Student B. Listen to Student B and write the letters.

BBC   **USA**   *VIP*   FAQ   OK

Lesson 2.1

7 A Student A: look at the photos of your friends. Complete the notes below.

1
Name:
Nationality:
Job:
Where is he now?

2
Names:
Nationalities:
Jobs:
Where are they now?

B Work with other students. Cover your notes and talk about the photos.

Lesson 2.2

8 A Student A: look at the information below. Write questions to find the missing information.

1 How old is Jakub Tomassi?
2 What's his …?

Jakub Tomassi, [1]_____ (age), and Julia Tomassi, 35, are husband and wife. Jakub is [2]_____ (nationality) and Julia is from Canada. Their business is in [3]_____ (city), and they're taxi drivers. Their company name is [4]_____ (name) and their special taxi-bus is good for families and big groups.

Jon and Liz [5]_____ (surname) are brother and sister, and their Moroccan restaurant, *Rocco*, is in [6]_____ (country). They're not from Morocco, they're from England, but their restaurant is very good for Moroccan food.

B Work in pairs and take turns. Ask and answer the questions.

A: *How old is Jakub Tomassi?*
B: *He's 38. How old is Julia Tomassi?*
A: *She's 35.*

Lesson 3.3

7 Student A: you are the waiter. Take the customer's order.

MENU
€2.60   €2.40
€2.50   €1.75
€3.25   €3.90

Consolidation 4: Units 7–8

4 A Students A and B: work in pairs. Read the situation and answer the questions.

On Monday at half past one in the afternoon there was a robbery at a clothes shop. You were the robbers! You said you were at a restaurant, but you weren't.

1 Where was the robbery?
2 Where were the robbers?
3 Were you at the restaurant?

B Work in pairs and write answers to the police's questions. Do not tell the truth!

1 What time did you arrive at the restaurant?
2 What was the name of the restaurant?
3 What type of restaurant was it?
4 What did you eat?
5 How much did it cost?

C Work with a police officer and answer the police's questions.

D Student A and Student B: compare your answers. How many of your answers were different?

Lesson 4.3

5 A Student B: look at the information. Write the events and times that Student A suggests.

Saturday	Sunday
10.15a.m. – film	9.30a.m. – festival
2.00p.m. – football match	
	8.15p.m. – concert

A: *Do you want to see a film on Saturday!*
B: *What time does it start?*
A: *It starts at quarter past ten.*
B: *In the morning? OK! Let's go.*

B Ask Student A to come to your events.

B: *Do you want to go to a football match on Saturday?*

Lesson 3.2

8 Student A: ask and answer questions to compare your picture with Student B's. Don't look at Student B's picture. Find six differences between the pictures.

A: *In your picture, is Bai's jacket black?*
B: *No, it isn't. It's …*

Lesson 4.2

6 A Student A: work with another Student A and look at the pictures about Yoshi. Say five things about Yoshi.

He studies English.

Lesson 9.3

5 C Student A: ask Student B the questions.

1 Where were you this time last year?
2 What was your first teacher's name?
3 Spell your first name backwards (e.g. *John*: n-h-o-J).
4 What would you like for your next meal?

COMMUNICATION BANK

Lesson 1.2

6 A Student B: write two *yes/no* questions about each photo D–F. Ask about jobs and places.

Photo D: Is he a doctor? Is he from China?   Photo F: Is it in Mexico?

A

Yolanda is from England. She's a sports teacher.

B

Marcos is a taxi driver from Argentina.

C

It's the city of San Francisco, in the USA.

D

E

F

B Listen to Student A and answer questions about photos A–C.

C Ask Student A your questions about photos D–F.

Lesson 1.3

2 A Student B: listen to Student A and write the letters. Read the letters below to Student A.

DVD   (EU)   www   IBM   **UK**

Lesson 2.1

7 A Student B: look at the photos of your friends. Complete the notes below.

1

2

1

Name:
Nationality:
Job:
Where is she now?

2

Names:
Nationalities:
Jobs:
Where are they now?

B Work with other students. Cover your notes and talk about the photos.

Lesson 2.2

8 A Student B: look at the information below. Write questions to find the missing information.

1 *How old is Julia Tomassi?*
2 *Where is she …?*

Jakub Tomassi, 38, and Julia Tomassi, 1_____ (age), are husband and wife. Jakub is Polish and Julia is from 2_____ (country). Their business is in Warsaw, and they're 3_____ (jobs). Their company name is *Koło* and their special taxi-bus is good for families and big groups.

Jon and Liz Henderson are brother and sister, and their Moroccan restaurant, 4_____ (name), is in Scotland. They're not from Morocco, they're from 5_____ (country), but their restaurant is very good for Moroccan food.

B Work in pairs and take turns. Ask and answer the questions.

A: *How old is Jakub Tomassi?*
B: *He's 38. How old is Julia Tomassi?*
A: *She's 35.*

Lesson 5.3

6 B Student B: you are a hotel receptionist. Read the information and answer Student A's questions.

HOTEL INFORMATION

Hotel money exchange at reception:
8.30a.m.–12.30p.m. and 4.30p.m.–6.30p.m.

Lunch:
hotel café: 12p.m.–3p.m.

Guided walking tour of the town:
9.30a.m., 12.30p.m., 3.30p.m. €35.

Café Slavia:
8a.m.–11p.m.

Opera at the National Theatre:
8p.m., €40

Lesson 10.1

6 B

Section A: 10+ points. You're good at the arts, so maybe the best job for you is a singer, an actor, a dancer or a musician. But maybe you don't like singing and dancing in front of a lot of people. That's OK, you can teach other people.

Section B: 10+ points. OK, you're active and sporty, but there aren't a lot of jobs for sportsmen or women. You can play sports at the weekend and get a job in the week teaching sports in a school or a gym. Or maybe you can be a salesperson in a sports shop.

Section C: 10+ points. You're good with your head. Maybe an office job is best for you, but do you like working with people? Then how about a job in a bank or as a manager in a big company? Do you like working alone? Then maybe a job with computers is good for you.

10+ points in no sections? Don't worry, there's a job for you ... but we can't tell you what it is! What job would you like?

Lesson 3.2

8 Student B: ask and answer questions to compare your picture with Student A's. Don't look at Student A's picture. Find six differences between the pictures.

B: In your picture, are Paul's trousers black?
A: No, they aren't. They're ...

Lesson 6.1

6 Student A: ask and answer questions to compare your picture with Student B's. Don't look at Student B's picture. Find five differences between the two pictures.

A: Are there two hotels in your picture?   B: No, there's one hotel. That's one difference!

Lesson 7.4

3 D Work in groups. Put the events on the timeline. Use the key phrases from page 81 to help.

a) The London Olympics
b) The end of the Berlin Wall
c) The Football World Cup was in Brazil
d) Russian Yuri Gagarin was the first man in space
e) September 11 terrorist attacks in the USA
f) Michael Jackson died

1961   1989   1997   2001   2009   2012   2014

E Turn to page 152 to check your answers.

Lesson 6.1

6 Student B: ask and answer questions to compare your picture with Student A's. Don't look at Student A's picture. Find five differences between the two pictures.

A: Are there two hotels in your picture? *B: No, there's one hotel. That's one difference!*

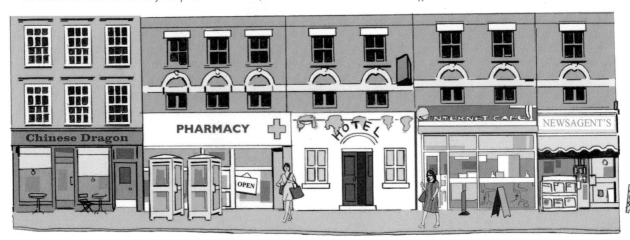

Lesson 6.2

5 A Student A: answer Student B's questions about Sydney and London.

B: Is there a train from the airport to Sydney?
A: Yes, there is. It's fifteen dollars.

	Sydney	London (Heathrow)
train / from the airport?	A$15	£21 express, £9.50 regular
underground?	no	£6
airport bus?	A$18	£15
other information?	taxi A$30	taxi £45–70

B Change roles. Ask Student B questions to complete the information for Barcelona and Hong Kong.

A: Is there a train from the airport to Barcelona?
B: Yes, there is. It's four euros.

	Barcelona	Hong Kong
train / from the airport?		
underground?		
airport bus?		
other information?		

C What's the best way to go from the airport to the centre in these four cities?

Lesson 5.3

6 C Student A: you are a hotel receptionist. Read the information and answer Student B's questions.

HOTEL INFORMATION

Hotel money exchange at reception:
9.30a.m.–12.30p.m. and
3.30p.m.–8.30p.m.

Lunch:
hotel café: 11.30a.m.–3.30p.m.

Guided walking tour of the town:
10a.m., 1.15p.m., 6.30p.m.,
€25 (evening €35)

Café Milena:
10a.m.–8p.m.

Opera at the Prague State Opera:
7p.m., €60

Lesson 7.4

Key to timeline

1961 Russian Yuri Gagarin was the first man in space

1989 The end of the Berlin Wall

2001 September 11 terrorist attacks in the USA

2009 Michael Jackson died

2012 The London Olympics

2014 The Football World Cup was in Brazil

Lesson 3.3

7 Student B: you are the customer. You have twelve euros. Order food and drink for two people.

Lesson 6.3

6 A Student B: you work in the ticket office at the central bus station in Bogotá, Colombia. Look at the information and answer Student A's questions.

>>> BOGOTÁ TO MEDELLIN BUS SERVICE <<<

TICKET PRICES			
Single	60,000 pesas		
Return	110,000 pesas		
TIMES			
Departure	8a.m.	11a.m.	1p.m.
Arrival	5p.m.	8p.m.	10p.m.
Gate	15	11	13

>>> BOGOTÁ TO MEDELLIN BUS SERVICE <<<

B Change roles. Student B: You are at the central train station in Istanbul, Turkey. It's 8.30a.m. You want to buy a ticket to Sofia, Bulgaria. Ask Student A questions to complete your notes.

ticket: a single to Sofia
price:
time of next train:
arrival time:
platform:

Lesson 4.2

6 A Student B: work with another Student B and look at the pictures about Daniel. Say five things about Daniel.

He studies Chinese.

Lesson 9.3

5 C Student B: ask Student A the questions.
1 What's your favourite colour?
2 Count backwards from 10–1.
3 Where were you this time last week?
4 Would you like a cat?

Consolidation 1: Units 1–2

5 Student A: look at the table and ask questions to complete the information.

First name	[1]Haru	[2]Fatimah	[3]Lukas and Katja
Surname	Nakamura		Fischer
Nationality		British	
Age	28		23 and 20
Job		nurse	
Email address	33haru@bnet.com	faha@bnet.com	

B: *Number one is Haru. What's his surname?*
A: *Nakamura.*
B: *How do you spell it?*
A: *N-A-K-A-M-U-R-A. What's his nationality?*

AUDIO SCRIPTS

Unit 1 Recording 1

Conversation 1

D = Diana   C = Carmen

D: Hello, I'm Diana
C: Hi, I'm Carmen.
D: Nice to meet you.
C: You too.
D: Where are you from?
C: I'm from Spain.
D: Oh, where in Spain?
C: From Madrid.

Conversation 2

T = Tom   K = Katie

T: Hi, I'm Tom.
K: Hi, I'm Katie.
T: Nice to meet you.
K: You too.
T: Are you from Ireland?
K: Yes, I am.
T: Oh, where in Ireland?
K: From Dublin.

Conversation 3

J = James   S = Steve

J: Hi, I'm James.
S: Hello, I'm Steve.
J: Nice to meet you.
S: You too.
J: Where are you from?
S: I'm from Australia
J: Oh. Are you from Sydney?
S: No, I'm not. I'm from Melbourne.

Unit 1 Recording 9

Conversation 1

R = Receptionist   M = Michael

R: OK, what's your surname?
M: Thompson, T-H-O-M-P-S-O-N
R: Ah-huh. And what's your first name?
M: Michael.
R: How do you spell that?
M: M-i-c-h-a-e-l.
R: Ah yes, for the fitness class in room ten.
M: That's right.
R: What's your phone number?
M: Er … it's oh five three two, four one nine.
R: And what's your email address?
M: It's mike at bmail dot com.
R: OK, thank you.

Conversation 2

R = Receptionist   A = Allen

R: Good morning. Can I help you?
A: Yes. My name's Byrne. Allen Byrne.
R: How do you spell that?
A: B-y-r-n-e.
R: B-y-r-n-e.
A: Yes.
R: And your first name?
A: It's Allen.
R: A-l-l … is it a-n?
A: No, e. E as in England. A-l-l-e-n.
R: Thanks. OK, here's your visitor's name badge. The conference is in room 379.
A: Thank you.
R: You're welcome.

Conversation 3

R = Receptionist   A = Anabella

R: Can I help you?
A: Yes, I'm a student, a new student.
R: Oh, welcome to the school. What's your surname?
A: Almeida.

R: How do you spell Almeida?
A: A-l-m-e-i-d-a.
R: And what's your first name?
A: Anabella.
R: OK, Anabella. Here's your student card.
A: Thank you. Oh, my first name's wrong.
R: Oh, sorry. How do you spell it?
A: It's Anabella, A-n-a-b-e-l-l-a.
R: A-n-a-b-e-l-l-a.
A: That's right.
R: OK, Anabella. You're in room 124.
A: 124?
R: Yes.

Unit 1 Recording 12

M = Man   C = Catarina

M: So, your name's Catherine?
C: No, it's Catarina.
M: Catarina?
C: Yes, it's an Italian name. I'm from Italy.
M: Yeah? Where in Italy?
C: I'm from Positano.
M: Positano! I don't know it. Is it big?
C: No, it isn't. It's very small. Very small and very old. Look. Here is a photo.
M: Oh, it's beautiful!
C: Yes … I love it.
M: And um … what's your job?
C: In Dublin?
M: Yes, here in Dublin.
C: I'm a hotel receptionist here in the centre of the city.
M: Oh really? So English is important for you.
C: Yes, of course. In my job I speak English, and I also speak German and Italian of course. Italian people visit Dublin a lot. They love it.
M: And you? Do you like Dublin?
C: Oh, yes. I really love it here.
M: Why? What's good about it?
C: Well, The countryside here is very beautiful, with mountains, rivers and the sea. And the villages are old and beautiful. I really love it here. And you … are you Irish?
M: Yes, but not from Dublin I'm from a small town in County Wexford.

Unit 2 Recording 2

M = Man   L = Lucy

Conversation 1

M: Hi, Lucy. Coffee?
L: No thanks.
M: Hey, photos. Let's see …
L: Yes, from the weekend.
M: Uh uh. Is this your family?
L: Yes, me, my husband, my son Johnny and my daughter Amy.
M: How old are they?
L: Erm, Johnny's three and Amy's six.
M: Where are you?
L: We're in the park.
M: Great photo. Lovely family.
L: Thanks. It's Johnny's first time on a bike …

Conversation 2

L: … and this is a photo of the children.
M: Oh, it's a great picture.
L: Yeah.
M: Let's see. This is, erm, Amy?
L: Yes, that's right.
M: And Johnny …
L: Yes …
M: … and in the middle? Your other daughter?
L: Yes. Jennifer. She's ten now.
M: Oh. And Jennifer and Amy, are they at the same school?

L: No, they aren't, Jennifer's at a special music school. Violin, piano …
M: Really? Wow, a real musician.
L: Well, she's only ten, so …
M: But that's great. And the other children?
L: Amy's on the football team …

Conversation 3

L: This is Tim …
M: Your husband.
L: Yeah. And Johnny.
M: Is Tim British?
L: Oh yes, he's from Cambridge.
M: And you, you aren't British. You're from China right?
L: No, I'm from the US.
M: Oh …
L: My father's Chinese and my mother's America
M: I see. Interesting. Erm, is your husband a businessman?
L: Yes, he's in the hotel and restaurant business
M: Oh. What's his job?
L: He's a hotel manager.
M: Oh, what's the name of the hotel?

Unit 2 Recording 4

1 We're from England.
2 They're actors.
3 We're in Japan.
4 You're right.
5 We're in class.
6 They're here.

Unit 2 Recording 11

Conversation 1

S1 = Student 1   S2 = Student 2

S1: Good class.
S2: Yes, very good.
S1: I'm hungry.
S2: Yeah, me too. Let's eat something.
S1: OK. Where?
S2: Erm … that Italian café? What's its name?
S1: Lugo?
S2: Yeah, that's right. Let's go to Café Lugo.
S1: OK, good idea.

Conversation 2

L = Lena   K = Ken

L: Hello, are you Mr Tajima?
K: Yes.
L: I'm Lena Smith.
K: Oh, hello. Nice to meet you Ms Smith.
L: And you. Please call me Lena.
K: OK, Lena. And I'm Ken.
L: Let's sit down. Coffee?
K: Erm … Yes, please.

Conversation 3

W = Woman   M = Man

W: Let's have a break.
M: Good idea. I'm tired
W: Me too.
M: … and hot.
W: Yeah. Let's stop.
M: Yeah, OK. Let's have a drink.
W: OK.

Unit 2 Recording 12

1 Let's <u>eat</u> something.
2 Let's sit <u>down</u>.
3 Let's have a <u>break</u>.
4 Let's <u>stop</u>.
5 Let's have a <u>drink</u>.

Unit 2 Recording 13

M = Man   W = Woman

Let's have a break.
Good idea.

Let's sit down.
OK.

Let's have a coffee.
OK.

Let's eat something.
OK.

Let's go.
Great.

Let's stop.
Yes, let's.

Unit 2 Recording 14

W = Woman   M = Man

OK, five people in my life.
Yeah, who's first?
The first is Duncan. Duncan's my brother.
How old is he?
He's thirty-one, and he's a businessman.
And Sarah … Who is she?
Sarah's a very good friend, my best friend really.
Where's she from?
She's from Scotland and she's a teacher.
Uh-huh …
We're on the phone a lot! She's great.
Nice. And Mark? Who is Mark?
Mark is from work. I'm an office worker and
rk's my manager.
Is he friendly?
Yes, he's very nice, very friendly.
Um, and Wendy?
Wendy is in my class. We are in a Spanish class
gether.
Who's your teacher?
Her name's Rosa. She's from Madrid in Spain.
ndy and I sit together in the class and now
're friends.
Is your class good?
Yes, the *class* is good … but our Spanish isn't
ry good!

Consolidation 1 Recording 1

Conversation 1

Tony   H = Haru

Hello, I'm Tony Morelli.
Hi, I'm Haru Nakamuru.
Nice to meet you.
You too. Is Morelli an Italian name?
Yes, it is, but I'm American.
I see.
And are you from China?
No, Haru is a Japanese name. My parents are
m Japan. It's good music, yeah?
Yeah, it's good. The singer is my friend …

Conversation 2

Fatimah   T = Terry

Hi, I'm Fatimah.
Hello, my name's Terry. Terry Gonzales.
Nice to meet you.
You too. Is Fatimah your surname or your first
me?

F: It's my first name. It's an Arabic name.
T: Oh. Where are you from?
F: My father's from Egypt, but I'm English. And
you? Is Gonzales a Spanish name?
T: Yes, it is but I'm not from Spain, I'm from
Colombia.
F: Oh, where in Colombia?
T: Bogotá.
F: Hey, I'm hungry.
T: Me too. Let's go and eat something.
F: Good idea. So, what …

Conversation 3

B = Brad   S = Sue

B: Brad Churchill, nice to meet you.
S: Sue Takahashi. Nice to meet you, too.
B: Your English is very good!
S: Thanks, but I'm from the US.
B: Oh, I'm sorry. But Takahashi is a Japanese name.
S: Yes, my family is from Japan, but I'm American.
B: Ah. Yes, my name's Churchill, very English! But
I'm Australian, from Sydney.
S: Oh, I know Sydney.
B: Really? Hey, let's go and have a coffee.
S: OK, yeah I …

Unit 3 Recording 2

Conversation 1

L = Leyla   N = Nasrin

L: Hi Nasrin.
N: Hi Leyla. How are you?
L: Fine thanks. You?
N: Yeah good.
L: Sit down.
N: Hey Leyla, what's that?
L: It's our homework.
N: For this lesson?
L: Yes, Nasrin.
N: Oh no!

Conversation 2

D = Denise   T = Tanya   S = Stan

D: Hi Tanya. What are those books?
T: Hi Denise. These books? They're for my English
class.
D: Wow! They're big!
S: Shhh!
T: Sorry Stan! Oh, they're not so big. They're really
good!
D: Who's your teacher?
T: Mr White.
D: Ah. He's good.
S: Shhh! This is a library! Please be quiet!
T/D: Sorry Stan!

Conversation 3

D = Dave   K = Kate

D: Hey Kate, what's in these two boxes?
K: My cups are in that box. My glasses are in this
one.
D: Yeah, this one's very heavy.
K: Yeah it's … Oh, be careful!
D: Oh, no. Sorry.
K: Oh, Dave …
D: Really, I'm sorry.

Conversation 4

O = Oliver   S = Sam

O: Wait a minute!
S: What's the problem?
O: Sam, is that my coffee?
S: This one?
O: Yes.
S: Oh, yes it is. Sorry Oliver.
O: And this is *your* coffee.
S: Oh. Let's get new cups.
O: Good idea.

Unit 3 Recording 6

Conversation 1

C = Customer   W = Waiter

C: Can I have a coffee, please?
W: With milk?
C: No thanks. Black.
W: Sugar?
C: Yes, please. One.
W: One black coffee with sugar! That's four euros.

Conversation 2

C = Customer   W = Waiter

C: Can I have two coffees, please?
W: Espresso or cappuccino?
C: Oh, espresso, please.
W: Anything else?
C: No thanks. How much is that?
W: That's five euros fifty.

Conversation 3

W = Waiter   C = Customer

W: Hi.
C: Hi. Can I have an egg sandwich, please?
W: White or brown bread?
C: Oh, brown bread, please.
W: Anything else?
C: Yeah, can I have one of those cakes?
W: These ones?
C: No, the chocolate ones.
W: Anything to drink?
C: Yes, a mineral water, please. How much is that?
W: That's four euros for the sandwich, three for
the cake and two for the mineral water. That's nine
euros.
M: Here you are.

Conversation 4

C = Customer   W = Waiter

C: Can I have a mineral water, please?
W: Still or sparkling?
C: Sparkling, please.
W: Anything else?
C: No, thank you. How much is that?
W: That's three euros.

Unit 3 Recording 7

C = Customer   W = Waiter

C: Can I have a mineral water, please?
W: Still or sparkling?
C: Sparkling, please.
W: Anything else?
C: No, thank you. How much is that?
W: That's three euros.

Unit 3 Recording 10

C = Customer   W = Waiter

Conversation 1

C: How much are those cakes?
W: These ones?
C: Yeah.
W: They're one eighty.

Conversation 2

C: How much is that?
W: That's four euros fifteen.
C: Fifty?
W: No, fifteen.

Conversation 3

C: Is this sandwich three euros?
W: No, it's two euros ninety.
C: Here you are.
W: Thanks.

Conversation 4

W: So that's two coffees and a mineral water.

AUDIO SCRIPTS

C: That's right.
W: So that's six thirty-five.

Conversation 5

W: That's eleven euros forty.
C: Here you are.
W: No, forty, not fourteen.
C: Oh. Sorry.

Unit 3 Recording 11

C = Customer   S = Seller

C: Excuse me.
S: Yes.
C: Where are those lamps from?
S: They're from Turkey.
C: Can I have a look?
S: Yes. This one?
C: No, that one. The blue one.
S: It's very nice.
C: How much is it?
S: It's two hundred.
C: That's expensive. Hmm. Fifty.
S: One hundred and fifty.
C: Seventy-five.
S: For you, a special discount. Only one hundred.
C: OK. One hundred.
S: It's a very good price.

Unit 4 Recording 1

I = Interviewer   W1 = Woman 1   M1 = Man 1
W2 = Woman 2   M2 = Man 2

I: Excuse me. Do you have a moment?
W1: Yes?
I: You aren't American?
W1: No, no, I'm from Japan. I'm on holiday here.
I: OK. So, my question is: what's different for you about life here?
W1: Um … well, here people live in houses … they live in big houses. I'm from Tokyo, and we live in flats, small flats. So that's very different.
I: … and so for you, what's different about life here?
M1: Um … well I study at university here. And it's very different from my country because here in the United States, the students have jobs. They work in the evenings, maybe ten hours a week.
I: And you? Do you work?
M1: Me? No, I don't. I don't have time. And in my country students don't work, they only study.
W2: What's different here? Um … oh yeah, people drive everywhere. I mean, they drive two hundred metres to the shops.
I: Do you have a car?
W2: Yes, I do, but I don't drive to the shops. Not two hundred metres! I walk.
I: And where are you from?
W2: I'm from England.
M2: I think it's not so different. I'm from Italy and my American friends are not so different from me. Er … we like sport … we like clothes … We, er … we go to the cinema, restaurants, have a coffee …
I: So you like the same things.
M2: Yeah, the same … not different.

Unit 4 Recording 5

M = Mia   P = Pete

Conversation 1

M: Hi Pete,
P: Hi Mia. London tomorrow!
M: Yeah! Great! Um, I just want to check the times.
P: OK.
M: Um. What time's the concert?
P: Let me check. It's at half past six. Yes, The Shakes … concert at the A1 … half past six.
M: Half past six. So do you want to go at six?

P: Um … Let's go at quarter to six. And erm, Mia, the food festival is in the afternoon. The international food festival.
M: But the afternoon is the party. Susie's party.
P: Oh yes. Um … maybe you …
M: No, the invitation is for Mia AND Pete. For me AND you.
P: OK. What time's the party?
M: From three o'clock to six o'clock. So that's only two hours at the party because of the concert.
P: So the party in the afternoon and the concert in the evening.
M: Yes.
P: OK. See you tomorrow at the station. What time …

Conversation 2

P: Good concert!
M: Yes, great!
P: Hey, Mia. You like Shakespeare, yes?
M: Yes. Why?
P: I have tickets for *Hamlet* at the Round Theatre, tomorrow.
M: Really! My favourite play! Afternoon or evening?
P: In the evening.
M: What time in the evening?
P: Half past seven. Seven-thirty.
M: Seven-thirty. That's good.
P: And in the afternoon … the food festival?
M: Ah, but tomorrow is the football. It's the final.
P: Oh yes. I want to watch that. What time is the match?
M: It's at quarter past two.
P: Sorry, What time?
M: Quarter past two.
P: Quarter past two. OK. Let's watch the match and go to the theatre after that.
M: OK. I'm tired. What time is it?
P: It's quarter past twelve. Let's get a taxi …

Unit 4 Recording 8

S = Sam   I = Isabelle   M = Milan

S: I'll go first. My question is about a), the computer and TV. The Amish family doesn't have these things. Do you think that's a good thing? Isabelle?
I: Well, for me it isn't a good thing.
S: Why not?
I: A computer is important for information, from the internet.
S: How about you Milan?
M: I think it is a good thing. I have a computer but I think I use it too much.
S: And TV?
M: I don't have a TV.
I: I do, but I don't watch it. How about you Sam?
S: I have both a computer and a TV and they're important for me. So for me, the Amish lifestyle with no computer or TV is a bad thing.
I: OK, my turn. My question is about e), the woman does the housework and f): the man has a job. A good thing or bad thing? Milan?
M: In my family, this is normal. I think it's OK.
S: Really? I think it's a problem. Maybe the woman wants to work.
M: Well in this family, I think they're all happy. Miriam is happy at home.
S: We don't know that. Isabelle, what do you think?
I: I think you're right, Sam. But … I think housework *is* a job. It's a very *big* job.
M: Hmm … Well, it's hard but it's not a job …

Consolidation 2 Recording 1

B = Beth   W = William

B: So if I press this …
W: Beth, who's that?
B: These are my favourite people.

W: That woman. She's beautiful.
B: William! That's my sister Alicia. Watch it!
W: Your sister? Oh … who's that then?
B: That's Keith. He's a good friend from universit[y]
W: Do you meet a lot?
B: No, but we email each other every day.
W: And this?
B: Monique, from work.
W: Are you friends?
B: Not really. But I like her a lot.
W: And if I press this … Oh, look!
B: Yeah, Paris …
W: … Cairo … and the Great Wall of China. Big traveller!
B: Yeah, then here …
W: Hey, nice dress.
B: You know that dress. My black party dress.
W: Yeah, I like that dress. Oh, you like the BBC.
B: Yeah, the website's great for the news.
W: Let's look at … What's this? Ice cream?
B: Yeah, from the Gelatino Café. I love it. But I don't go there a lot.
W: And what's this?
B: Johnny Depp.
W: Is he one of your favourite people?
B: No, but *Pirates of the Caribbean* is one of my favourite films.
W: And here's another film. *Pirates of the Caribbe[an]* two. Johnny Depp again and here's …
B: OK, that's enough …

Unit 5 Recording 2

Conversation 1

M = Man   W = Woman

M: How's the family?
W: Fine. Well, you remember Clara?
M: Clara, your daughter? Yes, how old is she now[?]
W: She's seventeen.
M: She isn't at school?
W: No.
M: Does she have a job?
W: No, she doesn't. That's the problem.
M: So what does she do all day?
W: Well, she listens to her music and … and she sleeps a lot.
M: What time does she get up?
W: I don't know because I'm at work. At the weekend she gets up at eleven.
M: Does she want a job?
W: I don't know. She doesn't talk much.
M: What do you mean?
W: Well, for example, in the evenings, we have dinner together. But Clara just sits there and listens to her music. Or she answers her phone and talks to her friends, but not to her family. It drives me crazy.
M: Does she …?

Conversation 2

W = Woman   P = Paula

W: Hi, Paula.
P: Hi. What's the problem? You look bad.
W: It's Julio.
P: Julio?
W: Yeah. Well, he doesn't listen to me.
P: What do you mean?
W: Well, I talk about my problems and he just checks his text messages or watches TV.
P: Does he talk to you?
W: Yeah … well, no … he says 'Mmmm'.
P: 'Mmmm'! What does that mean?
W: It means he doesn't really listen.
P: Oh, my boyfriend is exactly the same.

Conversation 3

M = Man   W = Wayne

M: Hey, Wayne. What's up? You look tired.
W: Yeah. No sleep.
M: What's the problem?
W: Neighbours. Problem neighbours. Or just one, the man in the flat upstairs.
M: Why? Does he play loud music? Big parties?
W: No, he doesn't. The problem is he works at night. He goes to work at six in the evening. I get home and I see him go to work every night.
M: What's his job?
W: He sells coffee in a snack bar at the train station.
M: And when does he get home?
W: About half past four. And then he watches television for two or three hours.
M: So when does he go to bed?
W: Oh, about six or seven.
M: And what time do you get up?
W: Huh! Now I get up at five. It's impossible to sleep. So I listen to music, drink coffee then I go to work around eight.
M: And when do you go to bed?
W: Late. Midnight or one a.m.
M: Ooh, four hours' sleep. Not good.

Unit 5 Recording 6

S = Miss Shannon   R = Hotel receptionist

S: Excuse me?
R: Yes, can I help you?
S: Yes. I have a reservation for tonight.
R: And your name?
S: Shannon.
R: Ah, yes. Miss Shannon. A single for two nights.
S: That's right.
R: I'm sorry. Your room isn't ready.
S: That's a shame. Am I early? What time is check-in?
R: Two p.m. usually. Your room is almost ready. Please have a seat.
S: Thank you. I have one question.
R: Yes?
S: When does the gym open?
R: It opens from six a.m. to ten p.m., except lunchtime. It closes from twelve to one.
S: Thanks. Oh, just one more question. What time is breakfast?
R: From half past six to nine o'clock.
S: And where is it?
R: Breakfast is in the restaurant.
S: Right. Thank you. The restaurant …?
R: Over there.
S: Right. Oh I have one more question.
R: Sure.
S: Do you have a hairdresser's in the hotel?
R: Yes, it opens every day except today, Monday.
S: That's too bad.
R: Yes, I'm sorry. But tomorrow is okay.
S: Tomorrow.
R: Yes, from ten to six. Actually, I'm wrong. On Tuesdays, it closes at nine o'clock in the evening.
S: Right. Thank you.
R: You're welcome.
R: Excuse me, madam.
S: Yes?
R: Your room's ready now. Here's your key card. Room five three eight on the fifth floor.
S: Thank you.
R: No problem. Enjoy your stay.
S: Oh, but I have one more question.
R: Yes?
S: I want to go on a guided tour of the old town. Do you know a good one?
R: Ah, yes. We do a tour from the hotel.
S: Great. When does the tour leave?
R: It leaves at nine a.m. and at three p.m.

MS: How much does it cost?
R: It costs fifteen euros.
MS: Right. Thank you. Do you have a map of the city?
R: Yes, here you are.
MS: Thank you.
R: Have a nice day.
MS: You too.
R: Any more questions I can help you with?
MS: No, thank you. Oh, just one …

Unit 5 Recording 9

M = Man   W = Woman

M: What's on your list?
W: Well, number one on my list is fruit.
M: Fruit? Why fruit?
W: It's good for you.
M: Do you really like it?
W: I like bananas and apples.
M: Bananas and apples. That's two things.
W: OK, fine. One is bananas and two is apples.
M: And what's number three on your list?
W: Number three is cake. I love chocolate cake.
M: Me too. It's on my list.
W: Maybe it's bad for you, but er …
M: Chocolate cake and fruit. That's OK.
W: Yeah, with fruit, it's good.
M: And number four?
W: Pasta with cheese.
M: Mmm … that's two.
W: No, I think it's one. I eat pasta every day. With cheese.
M: OK, pasta and cheese, fine.
W: And number five is cereal.
M: Really? Do you really like cereal?
W: I do, yes.
M: What about drinks?
W: Milk for my cereal.
M: Yes. And what other drink do you have?
W: I have tea. English tea.
M: Of course. Me too.

Unit 6 Recording 2

P = Pete   CA1 = Customer advisor   MG = Megan
M = Man

P: Excuse me?
CA: Yes?
P: Is there a train to York tonight?
CA: No, sorry, there aren't any trains tonight. It's the weather. It's very bad.
P: Not any trains? Not one?
CA: No, not tonight. Maybe tomorrow. They …
P: Sorry, excuse me.
MG: Hello? Pete, where are you?
P: Hi, I'm here in London, in the station, but there aren't any trains and … Megan, Megan …? Oh, no …
Excuse me, is there a payphone near here? My phone's dead.
M: Yes. There's a payphone over there.
P: Thanks. Oh, and is there an internet café?
M: Erm … I don't think so. No, there isn't an internet café. Not in the station but there's one in Judd Street.
P: Judd Street. Thanks.
M: You're welcome.
CA: Can I help you?
P: Yes. Are there any restaurants in the station?
CA: Yes, there are … but … what's the time?
P: Um … Half past eleven.
CA: Ah, they're closed now, but there's a café over there. That's open.
P: And is there a cash machine here?
CA: Yes, over there.
P: Right. And hotels?

CA: There are two hotels near here. The Charlotte Street Hotel … that's about two hundred and fifty pounds a night.
P: Two hundred and fifty pounds? That's expensive.
CA: And there's the Ridgemount, that's about eighty pounds.
P: Where's that?
CA: It's here on the map.
P: Great … thanks for your help.
A: No problem.

Unit 6 Recording 6

T = Traveller   TS = Ticket seller

T: A ticket to Amsterdam, please.
TS: Single or return?
T: A return, please.
TS: Leaving today?
T: Yes.
TS: When do you want to come back?
T: Tomorrow afternoon.
TS: OK. That's twenty-nine euros.
T: Sorry? How much?
TS: Twenty-nine euros.
T: What time's the next bus?
TS: There's one at half past two.
T: Right. What time does it arrive in Amsterdam?
TS: At quarter past four. Here's your ticket.
T: Thank you. Which gate is it?
TS: The bus leaves from gate twenty-four.
T: Sorry? Gate thirty-four?
TS: No, gate twenty-four.
T: Thanks a lot.

Unit 6 Recording 9

I live in Sao Paulo, Brazil but I'm from the countryside. Brazilian people love their cars, but it's difficult to drive in Sao Paulo – there are too many cars and it's very, very slow. There's a good public transport system and a lot of people use the underground or buses, and the suburban train. More and more people go to work by bike but I don't. I think bikes are dangerous in the city. The best way to travel in the city centre is by underground, but it's very crowded in the mornings. In the countryside, a lot of people drive, of course, or they use buses. In my village, I go everywhere by bike.

Consolidation 3 Recording 1

Conversation 1

C = Customer   W = Waiter

C: Excuse me.
W: Yeah.
C: There's a problem with my coffee. It's cold.
W: Oh, sorry. Let me get you another one.
C: Thanks.

Conversation 2

C = Customer   SA = Shop assistant

C: Do you have The New York Times?
SA: Sorry, we don't. We usually have it, but not today.
C: Oh. Well, do you have any other newspapers in English?
SA: We have The Times.
C: That's a British paper, yeah?
SA: That's right.
C: Hmm, no thanks. I really want an American paper.

Conversation 3

W1 = Woman 1   W2 = Woman 2

W1: OK, let's get some money out.
W2: What's the problem?
W1: It says there isn't any money in the machine.

AUDIO SCRIPTS

W2: Oh, no.
W1: Maybe it's because it's a bank holiday. Look, I have some money. Let's go to Salvatore's café. It isn't expensive.

Conversation 4

M = Man 1   M2 = Man 2

M1: Excuse me.
M2: Is there a problem?
M1: Yes, I'm in number three and the computer's broken.
M2: Let me see. Ah, yes, there's a problem. Please try number five.

Conversation 5

P = Pharmacist   M = Man

P: Can I help you?
M: Yes, I'm not very well. I'm very hot and I'm tired all the time. Do you have something to help?
P: These are good. Go home and go to bed.
M: How much are they?
P: Five euros.
M: Five euros. Hmm, no thank you.

Unit 7 Recording 1

T = Traveller   TS = Ticket seller

1 I was at home with my parents and my brother and sister. There was a family party, but nothing really special. There were fireworks on TV … but I think I was asleep at midnight. I don't really remember.
2 We were in Miami, Florida, at a concert. The bands were great – the Gipsy Kings and some other local bands. It was great.
3 I was at work in Sydney. I work at a club, and of course it was a very big night for us. The money was good. Everybody was happy, crazy. There were fantastic fireworks over the Sydney Opera House.
4 I was on a beach in Fiji with my friends. There was a beautiful sunrise. We were the first people to see the start of the year 2000. And we weren't alone – there were hundreds of people on the beach with us. It was a beautiful morning, very peaceful …
5 I was in hospital. I was born on January the first, 2000. My mother says there was a party. Maybe it was for the New Year … or was the party for me?

Unit 7 Recording 6

started   talked   arrived   played   waited
moved   tried   stopped   travelled   finished
wanted   asked

Unit 7 Recording 8

Conversation 1

M = Man   E = Emma   A = Audience

M: Hey, Emma, let's go!
E: What?
M: Let's go!
E: Why? What's the problem?
M: This film. It's terrible.
E: Really? I think it's all right.
M: Oh, come on. Let's go.
E: No, I want to stay.
A: Ssshhh!
E: Have some popcorn.
M: No thanks.

Conversation 2

M = Man   W = Woman

M: How was your steak?
W: Delicious, just right. I really liked it. How was your chicken?
M: Urgh, I didn't like it. It wasn't very good.
W: Oh, well here's the ice cream. Thank you.

M: What do you think of the ice cream?
W: Mmm. It's fantastic!
M: Yes, this is good.

Conversation 3

W = Woman   E = Emma

W: Hi, Emma. How are you?
E: Fine, thanks and you?
W: I'm OK. Um, were you at Warren's party yesterday?
E: Yeah.
W: How was it?
E: It was all right …
W: But … ?
E: Mmm. Well, it was boring – there weren't a lot of people there.
W: Ah.
E: So where were you?
W: Ah, well. I went to Adam's party.
E: Adam's party?
W: Yeah,
E: I didn't know about it.
W: Uh, sorry …
E: Oh. How was it?
W: Er … it was very good.

Unit 7 Recording 10

all right   terrible   fantastic   great   delicious
not very good   boring   interesting   awful
not bad

Unit 7 Recording 11

M = Man   W = Woman

1
M: How was your steak?
W: Delicious, just right.

2
W: How was your chicken?
M: It wasn't very good.

3
M: What do you think of the ice cream?
W: It's fantastic!

4
W: How was the party?
M: It was boring.

Unit 7 Recording 12

W = Woman   M = Man

W: OK, so which was first?
M: I think the first man on the moon.
W: Yes, I agree. But which date – 1969 or 1975?
M: I think it was 1969.
W: OK, let's put that. So, what was next?
M: I think Google started.
W: I'm not sure. Maybe the Japanese tsunami?
M: No, Google was before the Japanese tsunami.
W: OK. Um, which date?
M: Erm … 1987, I think.
W: Was there internet in 1987?
M: Sure. Well, I think so. Maybe.
W: OK. 1987.
M: And I think the Japanese tsunami was next, in twenty eleven.
W: Not two thousand and seven?
M: No, twenty eleven. I remember it well because I was in London at that time.
W: OK, so that's twenty eleven. And Nelson Mandela?
M: He died in twenty thirteen, I think.
W: Twenty thirteen. Right, let's check the answers. OK, we were right about three answers. The first man on the moon was in 1969, the Japanese tsunami was in twenty eleven and Nelson Mandela died in twenty thirteen.

M: But we were wrong about Google?
W: Yes. Google didn't start in 1987. It started in 1996.

Unit 8 Recording 3

P = Presenter   K = Ken   C = Clare   D = Dan

P: Welcome to *Good and Bad*. This week we talk about holidays – good holidays and bad holidays. Our hotline is 123 2222. And here's our first caller. Hello, Ken?
K: Hi.
P: So, tell us about your two holidays.
K: Yeah, well my family went camping in Canada when I was twelve. We had one tent for six people and we didn't have water or electricity.
P: Oh, right. Did you like it?
K: Yes, I did. It was … fantastic. No TV, no internet … we cooked on a fire and played games.
P: Sounds great. And your other holiday?
K: Last year, I went to Australia with my girlfriend to Surfer's Paradise. I lost my passport on the first day.
P: Sorry to hear that.
K: But the beach at Surfer's Paradise was beautiful. The water was fantastic. We went swimming and just relaxed … but then I ate some bad food … fish … and I became very ill. I was ill for a week.
P: Ow. So that was a bad holiday. But as you say, Surfer's Paradise is a beautiful place.
K: Yes, it is.
P: OK, Ken. Thank you for calling. Next caller … Clare? Are you there?
C: Yeah, hello.
P: Hi. Tell us about your holidays.
C: Well, last year we went to France, on a group tour.
P: Oh, where did you go?
C: We went to Paris, but … there was a problem with the plane. We waited for ten hours at the airport. Then they said there weren't any seats on the next plane. Or the next plane.
P: Oh, no! What did you do?
C: We went by train! We had five hours in Paris. We saw some interesting buildings and a museum, and then we came home.
P: By plane?
C: No, by train. We had dinner on the train. Expensive sandwiches!
P: So that wasn't very good. How about your other holiday? The good one?
C: Ah yes, it was in China. I was there for two months. I was alone, so I met a lot of local people. They were very nice.
P: Did you speak English with them?
C: No, I didn't. I spoke a little Chinese and they liked that.
P: Great. Thanks, Clare. And next we have Dan. Hi, Dan.
D: Hi.
P: Is your first holiday good or bad?
D: Good – really good. I went to Peru. It was a walking holiday and it was wonderful.
P: Why was that?
D: Well, I went with a friend and we …

Unit 8 Recording 6

SA = Shop assistant   C = Customer

Conversation 1

C: Excuse me, where's the fruit?
SA: Do you see the vegetables over there?
C: Vegetables? What are they?
SA: Vegetables … you know, tomatoes, potatoes, carrots.
C: Oh, vegetables.
SA: Yeah. Vegetables.

OK … vegetables.

: The fruit's behind the vegetables.

Sorry?

: You see the vegetables? They're in front of the it. Over there.

Let me check. The fruit's behind the vegetables.

: Yes, that's right.

Oh, OK. Thanks.

: No problem.

nversation 2

Excuse me, where's the bread?

: Er … Do you see the snacks?

Snacks? I don't know 'snacks'.

: Snacks, for example, chocolate, nuts and crisps.

Oh, I understand.

: The bread is on the right of the snacks.

Can I check? On the right of the snacks?

: Yes. Opposite the fruit.

Thank you.

: You're welcome.

nversation 3

Excuse me, where are the cakes?

: I think they're near the snacks.

Near the snacks. Which way?

: I'm not sure. I know the cereal is opposite the acks …

Cereal? What's that?

: Cereal. Like Corn Flakes.

Er …?

: Erm, for breakfast. You have it with milk.

Oh, OK.

: Yes, so the cereal is opposite the snacks.

OK, and the cakes?

: I think they're on the right of the cereal.

On the right. Thank you.

: No problem. Or maybe …

Thank you!

nit 8 Recording 8

is is my bad holiday story. Last year I went to waii on holiday. First, I missed my plane, so I ok another plane. I arrived in Honolulu one day e. The weather was very bad, and it rained for e first three days. I stayed in my hotel room and ad a book. The hotel was noisy because my om was next to the road. There was a restaurant, t the food was expensive, and it wasn't very od. I was there for two weeks, and I was very ppy to go home.

onsolidation 4 Recording 1

My name's Sara. I'm the receptionist in the hotel. Mr Black and Mr Brown went out yesterday afternoon at a quarter to two. They came back together … at about half past three, and they went to their rooms.

My name's Alan. I'm a waiter in the hotel restaurant. I was in the restaurant last night. There were two men and a woman in the restaurant all evening. One man and the woman danced for about half an hour – from half past nine to ten o'clock. They all left at ten o'clock.

I'm a guest in the hotel. My room is on the right of Mr and Mrs Black's room. Their radio was on last night from about ten to eleven. It was very noisy!

I'm the night receptionist. Mr Black went out at ten o'clock. He said he wanted to take a walk. Then at a quarter past ten, another man went out. I didn't see him very well. Maybe it was Mr Brown. I don't know.

My name's Mary White. I'm a guest in the hotel. I came back from the town at about half past ten. I saw a woman in front of the hotel. She had men's clothes: a man's jacket, a man's trousers and a man's hat. I was surprised, you know. A woman in a man's clothes. Was there a party or something?

Unit 9 Recording 1

1

buy   bought

I bought it for my mother.

2

sell   sold

I sold it on e-bay.

3

pay   paid

I paid ten dollars for a coffee!

4

cost   cost

It cost five hundred euros.

5

give   gave

I gave it to a friend.

6

get   got

I got it for my birthday.

Unit 9 Recording 2

1 A shopping mistake? Um … well my boyfriend wanted to go camping, so I bought him a tent. It was a good tent. I paid seventy pounds for it. Anyway, he put it up in the garden – once, I think. Imagine that, just one time! He never used it again. It was a waste of money. The truth is he really likes hotels!

2 I don't really know … Oh yeah, last year my wife bought me an exercise bike. I thought it was a good idea, too, but you know, I think I used it three times. It was hard work! A real waste of money!

3 Shopping mistakes? Oh, that's easy. Clothes. I often buy clothes and then when I get them home I don't like them. For example, last month I went shopping with a friend and I bought a hat. It cost a hundred euros. My friend said it looked beautiful. My boyfriend said it was terrible … so I sold it … on the internet. I got fifty euros for it. It was a real waste of money.

4 A shopping mistake? Oh yes, all the time. For example, I got my sister's little boy some drums, for his birthday. I thought it was a good idea. He loves those drums. He plays them all day. So he's happy … but my sister isn't happy. Now she doesn't talk to me! I phoned her yesterday, but she didn't answer.

5 A shopping mistake. Erm … oh yeah, my mother gave us a lamp. We didn't like it, but I know it cost her a lot of money. Then after a week I broke it. I tried to fix it but it was impossible. Whoops!

Unit 9 Recording 4

I love flowers.

We like going shopping.

He doesn't like flying.

She hates chocolates.

Do you like peaches?

Does he like getting gifts?

Unit 9 Recording 6

Conversation 1

L = Lisa   T = Tom

L: Hi, Tom. It's Lisa.

T: Oh hi, Lisa. How are you?

L: Fine thanks. Listen, what do you want for your birthday?

T: Oh, I don't know. Let me think … um, I don't know.

L: I'm in Bridge's Department Store, so it's a good time to tell me.

T: Um … well, maybe something from the World Cup.

L: For example?

T: Er …

L: Well, would you like a football shirt, or …?

T: Um … no. Oh, I know! I'd like a DVD.

L: A DVD of what?

T: Well, can you get me a DVD of the World Cup?

L: OK.

T: Great. Thanks.

L: No problem. Bye.

T: Bye.

Conversation 2

L = Lisa   SA = Shop assistant

L: Excuse me, Can you help me? Where's the Sports department?

SA: It's over there. Behind the Toy department.

L: Thanks.

Conversation 3

L = Lisa   SA = Shop assistant

SA: Can I help you?

L: Yes, I'd like a football DVD, but there aren't any DVDs here.

SA: No, the sports DVDs are in Home Entertainment. In the DVD section.

L: Where's that?

SA: It's opposite Computers and Phones. Over there.

L: Thanks.

Conversation 4

L = Lisa   SA = Shop assistant

SA: Can I help you?

L: Yeah, I want a DVD of the World Cup, but there are two different DVDs here. Which one is best, do you think?

SA: Erm … let me see … this one has all the important matches.

L: Can I see it? Oh yes. How much is it?

SA: It's twenty euros.

L: OK, can I have this one, please.

SA: Yes, you pay over there.

L: Oh, right. Thanks.

SA: You're welcome.

Unit 9 Recording 10

1 What's your favourite fruit?

2 Where were you last Saturday afternoon?

3 Do you want a new car?

4 What did you study in the last lesson?

Unit 9 Recording 11

One of my favourite possessions is my camera. It's very small, and I keep it in my bag. I bought it last year in New York. I like it because it's easy to use and it takes very good photos. I take photos of my friends, and of places and of me. I have a lot of photos of me in different places. I put them on my website. I travel a lot, and I usually travel alone, but my camera is my travel partner.

Unit 10 Recording 1

Conversation 1

I = Interviewer   G = Greg

I: So, Greg. Thanks for coming in.

G: No problem.

I: Right, I have some questions for you.

G: OK.

I: Er … first of all, can you ride a motorbike?

G: Yes, um … yes, I can. Of course.

I: That's good. And do you know the city well? Can you find a place fast?

G: Yes, I can. No problem.

I: And in this job you sometimes work alone …

G: That's not a problem.
I: … but you meet a lot of people.
G: I like people.
I: OK, good. Oh, and we sometimes get very busy and we need help in the kitchen – cleaning or cooking. Is that OK?
G: Yeah, no problem. I worked in a café last year and I made sandwiches … and pizzas.
I: Great! Can you start tomorrow?
G: Sure. Wow, I got the job?
I: Yes, congratulations! Come and look at the motorbike.
G: Oh, it's big.
I: Yeah, here you go. Try it.
G: Oh, er, OK. It's a bit difficult to ride. But I'm sure I can learn.
I: Be careful!
G: Aaah!
I: Oh, no! Greg, are you OK? Next interview, I think.

Conversation 2

I1 = Interviewer 1   M = Man   I2 = Interviewer 2

I1: So, you think this is the job for you.
M: Yeah, yeah I do.
I1: OK, are you good with people?
M: Yes, I am.
I2: And can you work fast? The shop is very busy with lots of people waiting for their planes.
M: I like that. Busy is good.
I2: Mmm. And what about the hours? The job starts at five o'clock in the morning some days. Can you get up early?
M: Yes, I can. No problem.
I1: Mmm. But this interview was for nine o'clock and you were late. You arrived at half past nine.
M: Erm, well. My train was late.
I1: Well, okay, um, we'd like to try you … for a month.
M: That's great!

Conversation 3

I = Interviewer   W = Woman

I: So, what languages can you speak?
W: English, Japanese, Russian.
I: Great. And can you drive?
W: Yes.
I: OK. And can you remember facts and information?
W: Yes, I can. I have a very good memory.
I: So, can you remember my name?
W: Er … Did you say your name? Erm … Sorry, I can't remember.
I: Oh, dear … OK, let's try some other questions.

Unit 10   Recording 3

1 Can you sing?
2 Yes, I can.
3 I can play guitar too.
4 Can you dance?
5 No, I can't.
6 I can't dance.

Unit 10   Recording 4

Conversation 1

I = Interviewer   T = Tom

I: Hi, do you have a minute?
T: Yeah, sure.
I: What's your name?
T: Tom.
I: OK, Tom. Can you look at this list? It's people's top ten goals in life.
T: Oh, OK.
I: So, do you have a goal for this year?
T: A goal? Yes, I want to learn something new. My girlfriend can cook really well, but she doesn't like cooking. So I'm going to learn to cook.

I: Mmm, that's interesting. Any special type of cooking?
T: Yeah, Japanese food. I lived in Japan and I love Japanese food.
I: I see, well …

Conversation 2

I = Interviewer   F = Fiona

I: So, Fiona, do you have a goal for this year?
F: I'm going to change jobs.
I: That's a big change!
F: Yeah, well, I work in an office, and I don't like it. I'd like to work outside.
I: Great.
F: My friend Sheila is going to help me.
I: Well, good luck with that.
C: Thanks!

Conversation 3

I = Interviewer   L = Liam

I: Liam, do you have a goal for this year?
L: Yes, I do.
I: So, what are you going to do?
L: Well, I work with computers, sometimes twelve hours a day and I often take work home. It isn't good …
I: Right.
L: … so this year I'm going to spend more time with my friends and I'm not going to take work home.
I: Great.

Conversation 4

I = Interviewer   R = Rudi

I: Rudi, what are your goals?
R: Er … I'm going to get fit. I never do sport. I can't play tennis or anything, but I'm going to start exercising. Something easy. Take a walk every day.
I: Sounds good.

Conversation 5

I = Interviewer   A = Alex

I: What's your goal this year, Alex?
A: I have two goals really.
I: Oh, and what are they?
A: One is to save more money. The other is to see my friends more.
I: That's great. And what are your plans, with your friends?
A: Well … hmm … maybe go shopping together.
I: Go shopping? Then you aren't going to save money!
A: Yeah, but I'm not going to stop shopping!.

Unit 10   Recording 6

Conversation 1

W = Woman   D = Duncan

W: Hi, Duncan.
D: Hi, how are you?
W: Good thanks. Hey, this is a great place.
D: Yes, it's really good. I often come here.

W: … well, that was delicious. Let's have coffee.
D: OK … wait, is that the time? I'm sorry, I have a lesson at two. Er … Here's some money for lunch.
W: No, that's all right. Keep in touch!
D: See you in two weeks, after the holidays, yeah?
W: Oh yes, that's right. See you then …

Conversation 2

M = Man   W = Woman

M: Excuse me, do you have the time?
W: Yes, it's half past four.
M: Thanks. So … erm … where are you going?
W: Me? I'm going to …

W: … so you're from Madrid. That's interesting.
M: Yes, well, I come from Córdoba. I moved to Madrid when I was ten.

W: I see … oh, look, this is my station.
M: Look, here's my card.
W: And here's mine.
M: Very nice to meet you.
W: Nice to meet you, too.
M: I hope we meet again.
W: I hope so, too.
M: Goodbye.
W: Bye!

Conversation 3

D = Doug   J = Jo

D: What do you think of the music?
J: It's not bad.
D: Hi, I'm Doug.
J: Oh, hello. I'm Jo.
D: So, are you from around here?
J: No, I'm not actually. I'm from …
A: … yes and I was in China the next year. I speak Chinese, you know.
B: Oh, really?
A: And I speak four other languages. French, German, Spanish …
B: I'm sorry, I can see an old friend over there. Nice to talk to you.
A: Oh … and you.
B: See you later.
A: See you soon..

Unit 10   Recording 9

Three years ago I bought a guitar. I wanted to learn to play guitar because I can sing and I like music. I tried to learn it alone. I had a book and I practised every day. I learnt some songs, and I played guitar and sang the songs. I was happy, b then my boyfriend said I wasn't very good at it. H said I needed a teacher. So I found a teacher, and studied guitar with him. The teacher was great but it was very different because he gave me homework every week. After four months I playe guitar really well. I still play every day

Consolidation 5   Recording 1

1 I want to learn a lot of vocabulary, so I'm going to learn seven new words every day. I like reading, so I'm going to look at the BBC news website and write down new words.
2 Speaking is a problem for me. In the coffee break, I'm not going to speak in my language. I'm going to speak in English. All the time!
3 I can't understand English very well, so I'm going to practIse listening. I'm going to listen my CD and read the audio scripts at the same time.
4 My grammar is bad. Very bad! I'm going to loo on the internet and do some extra grammar practice.
5 I want to improve my writing, so I'm going to write a diary every night, in English. I'm going write about my day.